CW00493592

STOP MAKING OTHERS RICH

HOW AUTHORS CAN MAKE BANK BY SELLING DIRECT

MORGANA BEST

BETTER BEST PRESS

Live to accomplish your own goals and dreams or be used as a resource to accomplish someone else's.

— GRANT CARDONE

CONTENTS

This book is written in
AUSSIE

centre

favour

recognise

AUSTRALIA

learnt

in the street

practise

judgement

travelling

optimise

sceptic

cheque

and LOTS more!

1. INTRODUCTION

> Progress is impossible without change, and those who cannot change their minds cannot change anything.

> — GEORGE BERNARD SHAW

Selling direct requires a complete mindset shift. Your author store is not simply another retailer. It can be, if that's how you want to start, but an author store can be so much more.

I realise the thought of selling direct and the ways to accomplish it successfully can be daunting to authors who have never sold direct, but it really is a join the dots process. The thought of it can be unnerving, like visiting the dentist. It's always better than you think.

Selling direct does pose challenges unique to authors. For a start, our products are low price and high volume. At least half our products are digital. And while our main market is generally in one or maybe two countries, our audience is international. It's hard to find information about selling direct for authors, and most ecommerce courses focus on dropshipping. And fiction authors and non-fiction authors face different challenges.

The strategies we employ when selling direct are not the strategies we employ when selling on the retailers. We need to approach selling direct as a business owner rather than as an author.

This book contains plenty of information, presents the benefits of selling direct, and sets out what is possible. I have a comprehensive course on selling direct on Shopify for authors who would like a detailed step-by-step process.

There is no magic wand.

I'm fond of magic wands. I write paranormal, after all. But if you're looking for a shortcut, go and look for the Loch Ness monster instead. It will be easier to find.

Authors often lament that they have no time to set up a store. The magic leprechaun won't set up a store for you. If you want to have a successful business, you will need to put in the work. It will also help to decide whether you want to save time or save money, as it's difficult to save both at once.

It's time to get the facts on selling direct as an author. I'm excited, and I'm sure you will be too.

2. PAY YOURSELF FIRST

66 Pay yourself first.

— GEORGE S. CLASON, THE
RICHEST MAN IN BABYLON

I have always loved books. For me, they were a
form of escapism. I was born before the Internet,
and as my parents were too strict to have a televi-
sion, books were my only method of escape. I was
an avid reader, reading anything and everything I
could. My favourite book as a child was Enid
Blyton's *The Magic Faraway Tree*. I also liked *The
Secret Seven* and went on from there to Agatha
Christie.

I loved animal books, but the animals usually died.
Very upsetting for a child. I suspect that's why I

now write cozy mysteries. Only people are harmed, never animals. It warms my heart.

So books are my thing, and the reason I sell direct is mainly for security, but also because I find it fun.

And this is why. And, as they say in the movies:

Decades earlier

My mother was from a wealthy, entrepreneurial family but married into the Closed Brethren. My father's extended family was infamous amongst the Brethren for being horribly strict.

We had to wear head coverings to church, which was not called church but rather a meeting, and we had to attend all the weekly meetings. We were not allowed to have friends from school at our house, and we were not allowed to go to their houses.

When I was a teenager, my mother decided to leave the Brethren. Her brother was second in charge of a religious cult, and she threw herself into that.

What does this have to do with selling direct, you ask? I'm getting to that!

In this religious cult, everybody was told to marry any random person from the cult. They said the world would end in the next few years, so it didn't matter who you married.

My sisters and I were sent off to a Christmas camp, which was basically a matchmaking effort.

Long story short, I ended up marrying a man from the cult. He decided to sink his money into a business venture and to save money bought a block of land with a small iron shed on it. It had a dirt floor, holes in the walls, and there were no facilities–it was an empty shed on a block of land a thirty-minute drive from the nearest small town in the middle of nowhere.

I had to live in the shed. It was a nightmare, as you can imagine, especially in winter when the inside water bottles turned to solid ice.

His business venture fell through, so he had to get a job. He drove my car to work, leaving me alone in the shed all day.

We were quite poor, so he left me a small packet of chocolates on a daily basis. That was my daily food ration while he went to work. He would eat at work and not bring any food home. I was always hungry.

To fast forward, I asked my uncle, who was high up in the cult, if I could get a divorce. He strenuously objected, citing fire and brimstone. However, he did concede that my then-husband could move to a capital city on a temporary basis. I was allowed to stay in the small town and have my car back so I could get a job and drive to work.

Glossing over what would no doubt make a bad movie, I ended up escaping. I moved to a town and got a job selling computers, commission only. It was just enough to pay the rent on a small one-bedroom apartment and buy basic food.

There hadn't been a job advertised—I had gone to the computer store and said I'd be prepared to work commission only. After the computer job, I went into another sales job after pitching myself and saying I'd work on commission only. Jobs were scarce in that town, and I had to live by my wits. Eventually, I got a job in advertising. In the time between leaving high school and going to university, I had worked for a well-known advertising agency as a copywriter.

My parents wouldn't help me because I was divorced. They didn't shun me—just gave me absolutely no help whatsoever and wanted me to get back with my ex-husband.

I vividly remember the first day I was able to go food shopping and buy a whole shopping trolley full of food. It was heavenly!

That experience made me realise the importance of financial security. Going hungry for ages is no fun. I had lived without any form of security for some time, and I was certainly going to make sure it didn't happen again.

I went back to university while working in sales for an unpleasant boss. Luckily, I was able to leave that job, and I eventually lectured at university, which I absolutely loved. A few years later, the administration at the university changed, and the new powers-that-be shut down several departments, suddenly leaving a whole bunch of academics out of a job.

Once more, I was out on my ear, but I was better off than my colleagues who had known nothing else apart from academia their whole working lives.

To backtrack a little, a national magazine interviewed me about my doctoral thesis. Soon after, Random House solicited my thesis to be turned into a popular book. The contract eventually fell through. I found it a stressful process, ending in

1993. I then decided to self publish, which was truly a dirty word back then. I paid for a digital run of 1000 copies and approached booksellers. I managed to get the book into the Collins bookstore chain. I also got my books—these were non-fiction books under my academic name, by the way—into niche bookstores.

Even earlier than that, when I had been living in the tin shed, I had written a book and submitted it to Mills & Boon UK. Mills & Boon wrote back to me with a list of editorial changes. They asked me to make those changes and resubmit. However, at that time I was in the process of escaping and lost the manuscript. These days, my pen name sells some of 'her' print rights to Harlequin (Mills & Boon is a subsidiary of Harlequin), so that's a dream fulfilled.

Fast forward to the Internet. I started a website in 2003 when my part of Australia was still on dial-up Internet. I still shudder at the thought! I shipped print copies of my books all over the world.

It was a template type of website, and it integrated nicely with PayPal, even back in those days. I did a business certificate course in person, and then did the Cory Rudl internet marketing course—they snail-mailed the huge, heavy book folders—and paid for a business mentor.

I forgot to mention. I had already sold the thousand copies of the offset run, and now I did a series of digital print runs with a big printing firm in Australia.

I sold direct to the public and also to specialist stores which would sometimes order hundreds of copies of books at a time.

About a decade later, I changed to a specialist ecommerce website that also integrated easily with PayPal. It notified me by phone when somebody put in an order.

But to backtrack a little again–I put my books up on CreateSpace in 2007. I started ordering books from CreateSpace rather than doing the Australian print runs.

I progressed to putting ebooks on KDP (Amazon's self-publishing facility) and then eventually Smashwords (an ebook distributor to the major retailers).

I became a full-time author in late 2010. Back then, Amazon had definite and pronounced cliffs: the 30-day Cliff, the 60-day Cliff and the 90-day Cliff. At each point, Amazon decreased their recommendations on the book, and there was a corresponding decrease in sales. Authors referred to these as cliffs. Amazon typically sent out an email about a new book 9 to 11 days after the book's release.

I went into Kindle Select when it started and received several Select author bonuses as well as Select book bonuses. (Kindle Select is where an author opts to sell the ebook exclusively with Amazon and is paid by pages read other than by the sale price. Originally, under the scheme authors were paid a fixed price per book.)

Then something happened that prompted me to go wide. (That is, also selling on the other major retailers instead of staying exclusive to Amazon under the Kindle Select scheme). Two of my books had been sitting on the Amazon store Top 30 for some time. One was under my own name, and the other was under my fiction pen name. I was excited to release the first book in a new series, expecting it would do well.

A few hours after the new release went live, it vanished. Like, literally vanished. It couldn't be found anywhere. I emailed the then Executive Customer Relations arm of KDP Support and was eventually told somebody had reported that my book had "illicit content." Yet this was a cozy mystery. There wasn't so much as a kiss in that book. ECR told me the book would take a few days to review.

The book did eventually come back on sale several days later. It had the most horrendous ranking, a ranking resembling a book that had been on sale for a week and had not had a single sale. I had released Book 2 in that series and it too was pulled from sale for several days. That killed the series.

I removed both books from sale.

At the time, similar things were happening to author friends of mine. Back then, fake reviews were rife. An author in my pen name's genre put sixty 1 star reviews on my pen name's book from fake accounts. The only reason I figured out what was going on was because those very same reviewer names put sixty 5 star reviews on the other author's book. I reported it, and all those reviews were removed from my book as well as the other author's book, but a week later another twenty or so 1 star reviews appeared on my book, and the same reviewer names left twenty or so 5 star reviews on the other author's book. This time the reviews were not removed. Go figure!

Anyway, these events happening one after the other plus the introduction of KENPs (when Kindle Select changed to paying for pages read rather than paying a fixed price per book) in July 2015 prompted me to go wide. All my previous financial worries flooded back to me, and I realised I did not want to have all my eggs in the one book basket. I had remarried, divorced, and now had 3 kids to support. I was the sole breadwinner.

Things typically change quickly in this industry, often with little or no warning, and it's always good to be able to pivot. I remember when Sony suddenly shut down their ebooks and eReaders, and years later, Macmillan shut down Pronoun.

When you sell direct, you're not reliant (either wholly or partly) on the major retailers. We've all heard stories of bots going wild and shutting down author accounts, and while most of these authors did get their accounts back eventually, the thought is enough to fill any author with dread, especially if the author is exclusive to one retailer.

Even if your store is only a small part of your business, it's a good form of security. If you have all or even some of your books in your store and something—heaven forbid!—were to happen to your main retailer account, you already have your books uploaded to real estate you own, and you have customers already buying from you.

And there's more! It's amazing what you can do with the right store, simply amazing.

3. DON'T BUILD A CASTLE ON RENTED LAND

> Don't build your house on rented land.
>
> — ANON

As independent authors, we are used to wearing our book business hats to some degree. We are used to engaging cover designers and editors, handling social media, and marketing and advertising our books.

But have you ever stopped to consider who benefits the most from all your hard work and effort?

If you were going to build a house, would you build it on your own plot of land or rent some land and build your house there?

Imagine you owned a small physical bookstore, but you also sold your books in a huge physical bookstore and some medium-sized physical bookstores. Where would you spend most of your budget? Would you spend your money fixing the plumbing or the broken shelves in your own store? Or would you contribute to the expenses of the bookstores you don't own simply because they sell your books?

Would you spend most of your advertising budget on your own store, or would you spend your advertising budget sending customers to the bookstores you don't own?

Sometimes, we as authors are blinded by our own little corner of the business world and don't stop to consider what is going on in the business world at large.

We put our time and effort into producing books, and then we spend money on Amazon ads, driving customers to the Amazon store. When the Amazon ad you are paying for sends customers to your Amazon product page, they are bombarded by images of other authors' books. Sometimes your book ads are shown on non-book product pages.

I've just looked at a random Amazon book product page. I stopped counting at 38 books—the main book from 1 author, and over 38 books that had nothing to do with that author's books.

The Amazon product page is Amazon's branding, not your branding.

For all your efforts, Amazon keeps around 30% of your money and to add insult to injury, pays you around 60 days later.

Sometimes there is a glitch with those payments. Some authors have lamented that Amazon emails to say their payment details are not correct even though they have used those same payment details for years. And it's not only Amazon.

I once changed my address details with Barnes & Noble and wasn't paid for four months. That amounted to several thousand dollars. I'm certainly not alone.

Recently, there have been reports from authors of Amazon requesting indie authors send them proof of rights for books they have written and published themselves. Now more frequently, Amazon removes a book from sale and then asks for proof of cover copyright image. These typically take five days to review while the book is removed from sale. A pity if this book has just had a BookBub Featured Deal or is on a bestseller list. It certainly won't be on a bestseller list after the five days have passed.

In June 2022, IngramSpark announced that Target would now charge an *accrual fee* and a *promotion fee* on books sold in Target starting at 5.5% of list price and increasing to 6% in January 2023. Of the promotion fee, IngramSpark said, "Publishers with books that are selected for a Target B2G1 or BOGO purchase will be charged a portion of the cost of the free item."

As indie authors, we can be forgiven for thinking that's just the way the cookie crumbles, and we have to grin and bear it.

And then there's the data. When we sell on one of the major retailers, we have no idea who buys our books. We have no way to get in touch with those readers. The major retailers keep the customers' data and continue to sell those customers other authors' books—or maybe other products that have nothing to do with books. By spending money on ads, we have driven those customers to the retailers. The retailers have those customers' data and can market to them.

We have no way to upsell to those customers. The retailer upsells to them.

The best we can do when selling through retailers is to get somebody onto our newsletter list.

Still, some of us have made six figures a year via the retailers, and others even seven figures a year. And despite the potential issues with having all their eggs in the one basket, some authors continue to make seven figures a year on Kindle Select.

Nobody is denying that there is good money to be made on the retailers, but what if you could keep most of that money for yourself and not have to worry that one of the retailers would shut down your account due to a wayward bot or would have an issue paying you?

Currently, readers are returning books after they have read them. TikTok encouraged this concept, and before that, Audible actively encouraged listeners to return audiobooks. Readers and listeners have been encouraged to read or listen to the whole book and then return it for a full refund.

Increasingly, authors are reporting a high number of returns.

And then there are the false accusations with account closure implications, most likely bot-driven. I myself received an email from ACX that I was no longer allowed to give out Audible codes due to recent misuse. However, I hadn't used codes for two years and had a comprehensive list of every reader who had ever received a code from me. ACX stopped responding to my emails after sending me copy/paste responses.

Numerous authors have had their Amazon accounts shut down for no known reason. In most cases, this has been a temporary measure, but these people have lost sales for at least several days.

In 2010, Amazon removed books from several erotica categories. In 2012, PayPal suddenly stated it would no longer pay authors for several erotica categories. Back then, PayPal was the payment processor for a couple of major author sites including Smashwords. The upshot was that many bestsellers were removed from sale, potentially threatening the livelihood of these authors.

As a result of PayPal's mandate, the distributor BookStrand removed all its indie books, no matter the genre, from sale. With no warning, Book-

Strand emailed indie authors to tell them they had removed the books from sale, would accept no more titles, had closed their accounts, and that the authors would be paid monies owed within 30 days.

PayPal eventually did back down, thanks largely to Mark Coker of Smashwords meeting with them.

Anything could happen to a retailer. They could go under, or at the very least, their policies could change. Kindle Select, for example, has gone through a few iterations with no warning.

In 2014, Audible suddenly cut royalty rates on indie-published books from an escalating rate of 50%-90% on exclusive titles to a non-escalating 40% for exclusive and 25% for non-exclusive titles. Thankfully, existing projects were grandfathered in.

Let's not forget that Amazon's original royalty rate was 35% royalties on all ebooks. On January 20, 2010, Amazon announced it would change the royalty rate to 70% for books priced between $2.99 and $9.99 (minus delivery fees) to come into effect on June 30, 2010. Apple was already offering 70% royalties for iPhone and iPod Touch apps and was about to announce the iPad. Apple entered the ebook market soon after with the iBookstore, and indie publishers were able to upload direct or through an aggregator such as Smashwords.

And speaking of $9.99, the $9.99 cap for the 70% royalty rate precludes us from offering big box sets on Amazon. The cap has been $9.99 for over a decade, never mind inflation. Jeff Bezos has been vocal about keeping prices as low as possible.

Low pricing is one of the core Amazon strategies. Jeff Bezos called it "permanent."

> At Amazon, I know what the big ideas are: low prices, fast delivery, and vast huge selection. Those are the three big ideas, and those ideas are permanent. Because they're never going to change, we can put energy into them, and the energy we put in today is going to be paying dividends later.
>
> — JEFF BEZOS

Amazon is a business. That's just the way it is. We can't take things personally. Amazon is not out to get us. Amazon makes business decisions for itself, and some of those decisions might not suit us. We simply need to make business decisions for *ourselves*.

Before Kindle, I was one of the many authors selling PDFs of my ebooks directly on ClickBank. I even sold PDFs of my ebooks on eBay back when they allowed digital products to be sold. I had an automated set-up for the books to be delivered by email. Back then, some of us were also selling direct from our own websites.

Then Kindle came along in 2007 and revolutionised the industry.

Now, over a decade later, there is a new revolution—authors selling direct from their own website or sales platform.

The selling direct method can be highly sophisticated. Shopify, for example, is the second biggest retail storefront in the world only to Amazon. Brands such as Penguin Books, Fitbit, Kylie Cosmetics, Hyatt Hotels Corp, PepsiCo, Sephora, and Tesla have Shopify stores. Aussies might be interested to know that JB HiFi's website is a Shopify store. Multi-millionaire

Davie Fogarty, the founder of the Oodie, has Shopify stores.

Covid isolation, too, accelerated online shopping and increased buyer confidence. People are happier than ever to buy online and to buy direct from the business owner.

When you sell direct, you have ultimate control. You can sell whatever you like, and you can bundle products together. You could bundle a paperback and an ebook and never go to a post office.

You could sell digitally narrated audiobooks if you so desired. You can sell whatever you like with nobody to tell you what you can and cannot do. You can produce a variety of print titles and not even have to ship them yourself.

You want to do a special illustrated print edition? No problem!

Want to sell low content journals? That's fine!

Better still, you get paid immediately. If a customer uses PayPal, that money is deposited into your PayPal account immediately. If you have a Shopify store, you can set it to pay you daily, weekly, or monthly (on business days). If the customer has paid by credit card, it might take the bank up to 72 hours to process this.

No more cashflow problems. No more waiting for up to two months to be paid. And no more waking up to nastygrams threatening to shut down your account for no known reason. No more constant quality control issues prompted by rival authors who make the most ludicrous suggestions which you still have to address one by one or Amazon will place a quality sticker under your book title.

I'm not saying you should have your books exclusively in your store and avoid the retailers. Certainly not! But you can now see retailers in a different light. Retailers can be a highly productive way to funnel readers into your store.

Selling direct is not a get-rich-quick scheme, but nothing about being an indie author is. The foundation is the same-old, same-old: write a good book, have a good cover, good editing. If it's genre fiction, make sure it hits the genre tropes. There's no shortcut, but if you build a brick at a time, you will have a good structure.

Sure, it takes work, but it's work that is putting money directly into your bank account rather than sharing it with one of the big retailers. Why subsidise a major retailer?

Selling direct does require a paradigm shift. As indie authors, we are accustomed to doing things one way. Now, there is another way.

RESOURCES

QUESTIONS

What problems have you faced on the retailers?

Would you face the same problems selling direct?

RESOURCES

Books

The 7 Habits of Highly Effective People, Stephen Covey.

Invent and Wander: The Collected Writings of Jeff Bezos, With an Introduction, Walter Isaacson, Jeff Bezos.

4. DON'T BE AFRAID OF CHANGE

66 They keep moving our 'cheese.'

— SPENCER JOHNSON, *WHO
MOVED MY CHEESE?*

The classic business book, *Who Moved My Cheese*, is based on a parable of 4 mice and the different ways by which they adapt to change. I love this book. It encourages people to anticipate change, to adapt quickly to change, to enjoy change, and to be ready to change quickly on a regular basis.

When you own a store, you are in a position to change swiftly.

Think of Covid alone. The pandemic certainly was unexpected and brought change to millions of people. Plenty of tourist businesses went broke. The construction, restaurant, hotel, and transportation industries, to name but a few, faced significant declines. Some businesses did well, changing to producing hand sanitiser and masks, for example. Other industries to do well were the health industry, cleaning, IT, remote work from home platforms, office supplies and furnishings, homesteading systems, delivery services, as well as the grocery, food, and beverage industries. The big win, however, was for online retailing.

> "A great entrepreneur is always learning because things change all the time."

> — MARK CUBAN OF SHARK TANK, BILLIONAIRE ENTREPRENEUR

Let's look at some changes to the publishing industry.

There have been countless, from clay writing tablets, metal writing tablets, wax tablets, stone, papyri, scrolls, wood-block printing, codices, hand-lettered manuscripts, to Gutenberg's printing press which started the printing revolution, from the industrial print revolution, print media, the electronic revolution, computers, to the digital age. And it won't end there.

Kindle's arrival in 2007 changed the book industry. Kindle Select started out as a paid-per-book system and then changed to pages read in July 2015. This happened with no warning. In 2022, Kindle Select did away with Author Bonuses, and also disbanded separate Author and Illustrated Kids' Book bonuses.

Kindle Worlds, writing fan fiction, was launched in 2013. Authors of the original content and Kindle World authors split the royalties. Amazon shut down Kindle Worlds in August 2018 although stopped selling Kindle World stories in July 2018. Amazon informed authors of Kindle Worlds' demise in May 2018.

The email included this paragraph:

> "As a reminder, please note that certain rights have been granted to the applicable World Licensor and, as a result, you may not be able to republish your work, use elements from the world, or otherwise exploit the rights you granted unless you obtain the World Licensor's permission."

— AMAZON EMAIL TO FAN
AUTHORS MAY 16, 2018

Some authors of the original content opened their worlds, while others asked their fan authors to remove all world information from their books.

Change is the only constant in the indie publishing world.

For years, indie authors could not do preorders. When Amazon finally allowed us to do preorders, the maximum preorder time was 3 months, and the preorder lockdown period was 10 days.

When I started, indie publishers needed a USA ITIN (often a real saga to obtain) or an EIN to publish. Now, we just need the tax number for our own country.

Barnes & Noble Press suddenly accepted Aussie authors in 2018.

In 2022, Smashwords merged with Draft2Digital.

Some social media platforms have fallen by the wayside, while others have risen.

There has been plenty of controversy about the advent of AI narration for audiobooks. Many authors are afraid AI will soon write fiction books, leaving authors redundant and broke. The writing is on the wall: AI *will* write fiction books one day. The subscription model is becoming more popular too. Are you in a position to adapt to these changes?

When changes in technology affect our industry, we need to see how we can work with that technology rather than simply lament. Who has a typewriter these days? Or a fax machine?

What happened when cars replaced horses? Pollution and the use of non-renewable fuels increased. The local economy decreased. When was the last time you rode a horse to the shops? Riots and strikes accompanied the introduction of electricity due to the loss of jobs as a consequence of power-driven machinery.

Technology giant IBM suffered losses in the latter part of the twentieth century as it did not adapt quickly enough to the rise of the PC. IBM reported a loss in excess of $8 billion in 1993.

Nokia invented the smart smartphone in 1996 but did not react swiftly to changes in software and apps. By 2013, Nokia held only 3% of the world's smartphone market.

Remember videos? I do. I remember hiring a video and grumbling if the person before me had not wound it back. In 2008, Jim Keyes, the CEO of Blockbuster, said, "Neither RedBox nor Netflix are even on the radar screen in terms of competition." Wow, what an example of *Famous Last Words*! Blockbuster stayed video-focused and two years later filed bankruptcy with a debt of over $900 million.

Remember Xerox and MySpace?

A few companies which have adapted to change include Amazon (which was once solely a bookstore!), Lego, Netflix, Spotify, and Coca-Cola.

Nintendo was founded in 1889 as a playing card company. American Express started out sending and receiving packages and currency in the Pony Express days.

The Corning glass company has adapted to several changes. It supplied the glass bulbs for Edison's electric lights. In 1915, it invented Pyrex, and sixty years later, produced fibre optic cables. Now, Corning makes the glass for iPhones, Samsung, and other smartphones.

The thing is, change is going to happen whether we like it or not. We can be a starving artist in the garret, crying into our no-brand watery soup, or we can be a businessperson and turn it to our own advantage. Those are the only two choices.

One of the great generals of history, Julius Caesar, said he turned every disadvantage into an advantage. This is good advice for entrepreneurs. Just don't cross the Rubicon.

RESOURCES

QUESTIONS

What changes do you predict for the book industry?

What can you do to position yourself to ride the tide of these changes?

TO DO

Scenario Planning.

Read up on Scenario Planning for businesses. Scenario Planning is a way in which a business deals with change by identifying possibilities about the future and determining how the business will respond.

RESOURCES

Books

Who Moved my Cheese? Spencer Johnson.

The Future Is Faster Than You Think: How Converging Technologies Are Transforming Business, Industries, and Our Lives, Peter H. Diamandis, Steven Kotler.

Author selling on retailers

Author selling on own store

Author selling on retailers	Author selling on own store
Lead Magnets	Offers
Reviews: ARC teams	Reviews: App/plug-in
Email marketing	Email **and SMS** marketing
Paid up to 60 days later	Paid at once
———	Influencer marketing
———	Cross sell, upsell
———	Customer data
———	Offer Bundles
———	Free store on socials and/or free shoppable pins: Facebook, TikTok, Pinterest, Instagram, Google
———	Abdandoned cart emails
———	Sell merchandise too
———	Tokengating

5. WHAT YOU CAN DO WITH A STORE

"Progress is impossible without change, and those who cannot change their minds cannot change anything."

— GEORGE BERNARD SHAW

With a store, you get customers. Obvious? Maybe not. People buying from the retailers are not your customers. They are customers of the retailer. When somebody goes into a Barnes & Noble brick and mortar store and buys a book, they are a customer of Barnes & Noble and not a customer of the book's author.

The general impression is that an author store is simply an alternative to the retailers—a buy button on at least one product. Nothing could be further from the truth. It can be so much more, depending on the type of storefront you choose.

Having a store requires a paradigm shift. You can't bring the same thought processes or systems across from selling on retailers to selling in your store. Having a store puts you in the business world rather than the author world. And these are worlds apart.

As authors, we are used to thinking that money is only made in the sale of the book or the sell-through to the other books in the series. When selling on the retailers, that is the only money accessible to the author, but with selling direct, money is to be made with cross sells and upsells. You cannot upsell on the retailers.

Having a store requires a mindshift. I will keep saying this. Context is as important as words for human understanding, and authors have the author-selling-on-retailers context. Selling direct is a whole other matter. For example, authors typically use lead magnets (tripwires), but ecommerce sellers use offers. With a store (spending on store and apps/plugins), you can have funnel offers or a single upsell offer on your sales thank you page. The post-purchase thank you page has 100% open rates. Why not make use of that?

Have you bought an ebook from Amazon, and on the sales confirmation thank you page it says, "Add Audible narration to this Kindle book." That's an upsell. Amazon does it, and with your store, you can do it too.

You will have plenty of automations to assist you in your own store. Think of your last online shopping experience. Were you offered entry into a rewards scheme? A prompt to enter your birthdate so you could receive a birthday coupon, gift, or card? Did you see a pop-up after checkout offering you a deal? If you abandoned your checkout, did you receive a series of emails offering you deals to sweeten the purchase? Whatever you experienced, you can offer your customers.

Email marketing is also different, and with a store, you can have SMS marketing if you so desire. SMS marketing eclipses email marketing's opening rates. Typical SMS marketing open rates can sit around 98% with a clickthrough rate of 35%. Text messages are usually opened within 90 seconds of delivery. In case you were wondering, you don't send newsletters by SMS, but you do send brief sales offers or launch announcements.

You know the Frequently Bought Together feature Amazon used for years on product pages? You too can do that! You can also use an upsell or post sell app with a one-click post purchase offer. These apps typically convert well and increase the average order value by offering at least one other product.

It's easy to offer the next few books in a series in a bundle. No, I don't mean a box set as such. That's so last decade! (Of course, you can sell box sets, but here I'm talking about upsells.) After somebody buys book 2 in a series, for example, you could offer the next 3 (or 5, your choice!) books at a discount. Amazon is now doing that.

Let's look at Facebook ads. Plenty of authors are lamenting that Facebook ads to the retailers have not worked for them since iOS 14. In February 2022, Facebook said that they expected the iOS updates would cost the company $10 billion in revenue in 2022.[1]

Authors who do not sell direct use Facebook ads for two things: running ads to their books on the retailers, and/or running ads to get people onto their newsletter list. These authors use Traffic ads and maybe also Lead generation ads.

It is important to note that ecommerce businesses instead use Facebook Sales ads (used to be called

Conversion ads), not Traffic ads, not Lead generation ads.

Sales ads are a whole different ball game. You
cannot use Sales ads unless you control the storefront, that is, unless your pixel is on the store.
Traffic ads and Sales ads are worlds apart. They
are polar opposites. Even audience selection is
different. With Sales ads, you can do all sorts of
amazing things such as advertising your entire
catalogue at once, retargeting, and re-engaging.

Facebook Sales ads are a major eyeopener for
authors who have been advertising their books on
the retailers or running ads to get readers onto
their newsletter lists.

Facebook integrates with both Shopify and
WooCommerce. If you run a Facebook ad
through one of these platforms, you will have the
data to tell you which sales were directly attributed
to that specific ad. It will also tell you how many
times the customer clicked on the ad before
buying. What's more, it will tell you the ad cost per
purchase.

If you're running a Facebook Traffic ad to one of
the retailers, Facebook's aim is not to show that ad
to buyers. It is to get you traffic as cheaply as possi-

ble, any old traffic. However, if you run a Face-book Sales ad, Facebook's aim is to get you buyers as cheaply as possible.

Shopify and WooCommerce are storefronts offering online retailers sophisticated tools such as payments, marketing, and customer engagement. Many of the world's biggest businesses use Shopify.

You can do all sorts of other clever things with a store. You can integrate with social media and sell on social media.

With Shopify or WooCommerce, you can have a free store on Facebook, Instagram, and Google. Shopify Analytics will indicate the number of customers who bought through Facebook.

With Shopify or WooCommerce, you can upsell and do a post purchase sell with an app. Most storefronts allow you to set up coupons or discount codes.

You get deep level data and analytics.

Shopify, for example, sends emails to people who have abandoned carts. If you wish, you can set up a sophisticated system with Klaviyo or another dedicated ecommerce newsletter service.

If you use a suitable email provider, you can even send emails based on somebody's buying behaviour. For example, if somebody has bought every book in one series, you can set up automated emails to suggest they buy a book in another series.

Most authors start with Payhip (see Chapter 16: 7 Ways to Sell From Your Site). This explanation is from Payhip's site: "Payhip is (an) e-commerce platform that enables anyone to sell digital products or memberships. Payhip - sell downloads, courses, coaching, memberships & more from one simple platform."

Payhip has the facility for customers to leave reviews, but there are review apps for Shopify and WooCommerce. These are automated. You do a brief initial setup, editing the number of days after somebody has purchased a product you want the review request to be sent. You can edit the already set up email template if you wish.

Then you don't lift a finger and just sit back and watch the reviews coming in.

In fact, Shopify or WooCommerce have apps for just about everything.

Various apps for Shopify and WooCommerce will track customer behaviour in real time, analysing and tracking what customers do as they move through your store. Shopify has a live view—you don't need an app for that. The app will record when customers add or delete a product to their cart, and which products they view, thus building a store user platform. This helps you improve your conversion rate.

You can sell bundles—an ebook with a paperback, a paperback with merch.

You can sell premium products, such as every book in a series, for a high price.

Why is this important? Ebooks are low price, high volume, which means we need more customers to make money. That is a challenge. If we have premium products available, we need fewer customers to make money. In simple mathematics (the type I like!), it takes 20 customers buying a $5 book to make $100, while it takes 2 customers buying a product at $50 to make $100. The cost of acquiring each of those customers might be the same. This is a challenge we as authors face.

However, authors have good imaginations and high levels of creativity, so we can think of ways to sell higher-priced products along with our books. Can you turn a character into an action figure? A toy? Anything with higher profit margins?

You could have a premium product. Not everyone will buy the premium product, but the ones who do will make it financially worthwhile. Here's a suggestion. If you have 100 books, sell them all as a $300 or more package. If you can think of a premium product worth more, that's even better. If you can bundle your book with a higher priced non-book item, even better still!

There are more opportunities to sell non-fiction than fiction, and if you are a non-fiction author, you could upsell to consultations and courses.

Multiple streams of income are important, despite the purists saying authors should only make a living from their books. Leave these starving-artists-in-the garrets to their own opinions, while you laugh all the way to the bank!

Selling direct, depending on your platform, is all pretty much automated, so long as you know what to do to set it up. Adding all your books can be time-consuming.

And while I think of it, yes, you can easily do assetless preorders and automate the system! All you need is BookFunnel for ebooks and BookVault for print books.

With Shopify or WooCommerce, you can sell print books without even touching the book, let alone having to go to the post office to ship it. This is all done for you with very little effort on your part. What you have to do is set up the product page on Shopify or WooCommerce and upload your files to Lulu Direct or BookVault. (Lulu Direct and BookVault each have an API which you can use if you have a different website.)

BookVault and Lulu Direct ship all over the world. What's more, if you are on Shopify and have Third Party Shipping Rates enabled, the shipping is automatically calculated. You never have to figure out any shipping costs.

Ever had website hassles? Have you ever discovered your Facebook pixel hadn't been working for eight months on your website? Or maybe that the contact form hadn't been working for ages? Did you have to pay somebody to set up a website for you?

With Shopify or WooCommerce, you can have a beautiful website that also functions as a store. People could go to your store and not guess in a million years that it's actually a Shopify store rather than a website as such. It can do everything a website can do, and it can do so much more. If you are on the Shopify Basic plan of $29 a month (when paid annually), that's pretty much what you will pay for hosting for a website.

Your Shopify store will have a contact form and somewhere you can place a privacy policy, terms and conditions, a fully customisable menu, either a header or footer or both, and the list goes on.

Have a look at my cozy mystery website which is also a Shopify store. morganabest.com My non-fiction site for authors is also my Shopify store. authorssellingdirect.com

Here are some other Shopify stores which are also author websites. There is absolutely no need to have a separate website. If you have some books in Kindle Unlimited, you simply create a product template with no buy buttons for those books and link directly to Amazon. You can sell your print books and audiobooks from your store.

You can even link to all the retailers on your product page if you wish.

samanthapriceshop.com

ruthhartzler.com

You can research and contact influencers, either directly or with the help of Shopify Collabs embedded in admin. Influencer marketing is a good way to drive sales. With your own store, significantly more options are open to you.

Another benefit of selling direct is that you can sell anything you like. If you can think of it, you can sell it. Your imagination is the only limit! You can sell anything you like and at any price you like. Want to sell a box set of 10 books in a series? No worries! Plus, nobody takes a retailer cut.

If you wish, you could sell special edition hard-covers exclusively from your store.

You could sell an ebook and a print book bundle. You could sell a coffee mug and an ebook bundle. You could sell a print book and a bookmark.

You could sell consulting services or courses. You could sell print-on-demand merchandise relating to your book subjects. A cozy mystery author could sell pet products or cozy household items. To use a cliché, the possibilities are endless.

If you have an entrepreneurial mindset, you could develop multiple streams of income from selling related products. If you are a paranormal author, you could add tarot cards, crystals, or fancy journals with gold foil sprayed edges. A children's author could sell toys based on a main character—or any related toys.

You can be on the cutting edge of ecommerce technologies and use tokengating in your store. More on this later.

You could, and most definitely should, upsell. If you're a non-fiction author, you could upsell a customer from an ebook to a consultation. The opportunity is there.

RESOURCES

QUESTIONS

In what ways would you do things differently selling direct?

Go to an ecommerce website and make notes on the offers.

What could you use as an upsell?

What products could you bundle? Think of 3 examples.

RESOURCES

Books

Rich Dad, Poor Dad, Robert Kiyosaki.

The 80/20 Principle: Achieve More with Less, Richard Koch.

Delivery of digital files plus Support

BookFunnel.

6. WHAT IS YOUR DESIRED OUTCOME?

> If you don't know where you are going, any road can take you there.
>
> — LEWIS CARROLL, ALICE IN WONDERLAND

People often ask me which storefront they should choose.

Instead of asking, *Which storefront should I choose?* ask yourself, *What is my desired outcome?*

What is your objective in selling direct? Do you want your store to be highly profitable? Or do you simply wish to provide your readers with another buying outlet?

Do you want to run a business? Or do you want to leave most of it to the retailers and simply have the option to buy direct attached to your website?

Running a business takes time and effort. It's not easy, and it is time consuming.

Which products will you sell: ebooks, audiobooks, print? Do you want to produce and ship special edition print books? Will you sell merchandise? Do you have a side hustle and thus products you can link to your books to sell? Are you a non-fiction author with related physical products?

Your answers to these questions will determine the route you choose to sell direct and also how you set up your store. Your answers will help determine your choice of storefront.

Buy buttons on your existing website are one end of the scale. Shopify is on the other end of the scale. At the risk of pointing out the obvious, everything else is in between.

Do you wish to throw yourself into it wholeheartedly? If you do, try to rearrange your writing schedule to free up some time to upload your books. It's like house renovating: it will take twice as long as you think.

Any author who sells wide knows how much time it takes to upload to all the retailers. Uploading all your books to a store will be horribly time-consuming. If you decide to start with one store and then change to another, you will be uploading all your books from scratch — that is, unless you move from WooCommerce to Shopify. There are migration apps to handle that.

Before I wrecked my ankle, I did distance running for years. There was a saying in the running world, "You're either a runner or a competitor." At any rate, we can apply this to authorpreneurism. Are you an author or a businessperson—or both? If you're an author first and a businessperson last, you might not enjoy selling direct.

There are plenty of levels to selling direct. You don't have to throw yourself into it wholeheartedly from the beginning if you don't wish to do so.

You could start simply by selling one ebook from your website. You could have anything from one book to your entire backlist of ebooks, audiobooks, and print, maybe even merchandise, as well as courses, consultations—and the list goes on.

It's worth repeating. You can have anything from a *Buy* or *Buy direct from author* button on your website for one book to your whole website being a store.

Payhip will deliver digital files for you and collect money. You could (I would say, should!) use Book-Funnel to deliver files and better still, provide support to your customers. Businesses pay firms to offer customer support, and with BookFunnel, you get it anyway.

There are various levels of stores and commit-ment. You could dip your toe in slowly if you wished. Nothing's set in stone. You could maybe start off with Payhip and swap over to Shopify later.

There's no need to feel overwhelmed. Seriously! Start off small and learn the ropes. Don't over-think it. Strive for progress rather than perfection. Don't spend money you don't have.

Think of ways to monetise your brand and grow your streams of income. There is plenty of opportunity.

Even if you start out small, consider where you intend to go with this. You might change your mind down the track, but it's like plotting. Unless you're a complete pantser, it's good to have an outline, and even if you're an avid plotter, things often change along the way. If you have a destination, it's easier to find your way.

It's a lot of hard work at first.

It's not a get-rich-quick scheme. There's no magic wand to make it all happen automatically. It takes time and effort. It's not quick and easy.

I was on the rapid release treadmill for years, and having a Shopify store has enabled me to move on from that. I was surprised when I was new to selling on Shopify, and other Shopify merchants mentioned they were glad it was Friday because they were looking forward to the weekend. Weekend? I hadn't had one in years.

Still, it's horses for courses. If you are somebody who loves the writing process and isn't too fond of marketing or any non-writing process, it will be less pleasant for you to have a store.

Costs.

Shopify Basic is $29 (USD) a month. (That's the cheapest for a store.) There's a discount for paying annually, which brings it to $312 annually.

That won't be a problem for an established author with a backlist and a newsletter list, as such authors can typically make money quite quickly with their stores.

But what if you only have a few books out? What should you do?

First, do you have an author website, and do you pay for hosting? If you do, what is the annual charge? If it's more than $312 a year, then maybe you could swap over to Shopify for your website. That way, you're not out of pocket, and you can sell from your website/store as well. It's easy to link to the retailers too. I mentioned this in the last chapter, with examples of Shopify-stores-as-websites.

If you are new to indie publishing and are not sure you should continue down that road, then maybe wait until your objectives have solidified.

Also, don't use money you don't have. Don't go into debt. Don't use credit cards. Seriously! Remember you get paid pretty much straightway when selling direct, so use that money and build on it. Use the free marketing options mentioned in a later chapter.

Whatever you decide, you can always change your mind later.

If you have a WordPress site and know how to set up a WooCommerce store, you could do that from the beginning. (I still recommend Shopify. That's where you find the 7 and 8 figure brands.)

If you're not WooCommerce savvy, let's look at the basic options. You could start with Payhip or Shopify Starter. Shopify Starter is $5 USD a month. It's a good step-off to moving to the Shopify Basic plan when you're ready.

Downsides to swapping to Shopify later?

Uploading 60 million books. You don't have 60 million books? Let me assure you, it will feel that way!

You won't have SMS marketing or an ecommerce newsletter list set up, so you will need to do that from scratch.

Still, it's quite doable!

Mistakes are fine. Just call mistakes "testing" - it sounds better.

It's a learning process. I've downloaded many apps only to discover they didn't suit the book business. Sometimes I tried several apps until I found the right one. That isn't a failure; it's a discovery.

Move on quickly, and don't stress about it. Accept it as part and parcel of the process.

> Strive for progress, not perfection.

— DAVID PERLMUTTER

Don't overthink it.

I've said it before. Don't put off doing it until you have it nicely clear in your head. Chances are, that will never happen. If you strive for perfection, you might not make any real progress. Don't be afraid to start, whether it's starting a store or figuring out an app. Jump right in!

RESOURCES

QUESTIONS

What outcome do you desire for selling direct?

Short term?

Long term?

Will you sell: ebooks, audiobooks, print, merchandise?

Will you sell: special edition print books?

Do you have another business you could link to your store?

Do you have any non-book products you could link to your books and sell in your store?

RESOURCES

Book

The 4-Hour Work Week, Timothy Ferriss

YouTube

Vanessa Lau's channel for entrepreneurship advice
youtube.com/c/VanessaLau

7. WHAT IS SELLING DIRECT?

> ““ The person who moves a mountain
> begins by carrying away small stones.

> — CONFUCIUS

Why send a customer to a retailer to buy your book? Not only are you cutting your profits, but you are sending the customer to other authors' books.

If you have an Amazon affiliate account, I'm sure you would have noticed that buyers will often click through on your book's link but rather than buy your book, will buy plenty of other products instead. If you directed the customer through an ad, you are paying for that ad and not profiting from it at all. Amazon is profiting from your ad and your money.

Having a store puts you, the author, in the position of power.

What is selling direct?

Selling direct means you sell ebooks, audiobooks, and/or print books direct to the customer rather than via one of the major retailers such as Amazon, Barnes & Noble, Kobo, Google Play, or Apple (whether direct to the retailers or through an aggregator such as Draft2Digital, Smashwords, or Publish Drive).

Selling ebooks on the Smashwords store is not selling direct. Selling on Etsy or eBay is not selling direct. These are not your own stores. That is like having a stall at a market where there are many other stalls.

If you have ebooks in Kindle Select, you cannot sell those ebooks from your website or from anywhere else apart from Amazon. However, you can sell the audiobook versions (apart from any audiobooks exclusive with Audible) and the print versions, as well as any ebooks not in Kindle Select. You could put books on preorder in your store and put them in Select upon release.

Apart from Kindle Select ebooks and any audio-books exclusive to Audible, if you own the rights, you can sell it in your store.

Do you have to be good at tech? No. (Not unless you do it from scratch such as WooCommerce.) I'm mathematically challenged and wouldn't have a hope of designing a website from scratch. My state doesn't have daylight savings, but I can never figure out the time in other Aussie states when they do have daylight savings. If you can upload books to retailers, you have the skill level to start a store.

It's like flat pack furniture but flat pack furniture with good instructions and not many parts. I'm not talking flat pack furniture where you have parts left over, and after you spend hours putting it together, it falls apart. (Speaking from experience.) Starting a store is very much A, B, C. It's simply following the steps. I explain how to do this in my course for authors selling direct.

The mindset is different. You have probably heard that selling wide and selling exclusively on Amazon are different mindsets. That is absolutely correct. Selling direct is a different mindset yet again. You will need your business hat. Once you start a store, you have truly become a businessperson, an entrepreneur. Sure, all indie authors are to some degree, but having your own store is next level. That doesn't make it hard, just different.

You will be able to, and most definitely should, develop a relationship with your customers. (Yes, your readers are customers. You can still like your readers—*customer* isn't a dirty word!) You will have to promote your store. Nobody will find your store without some effort as you are the only person to promote it. If you don't promote it, it's highly unlikely customers will find it organically.

You are the one to make all the corporate decisions.

The way you do newsletters will be different. You can get most customers who buy or download a book from your store onto a list with a pop-up subscribe form with an offer. There is then less emphasis on lead magnets and more emphasis on offers. And, of course, there is SMS marketing.

RESOURCES

QUESTIONS

Are you able to put your entire backlist in your store?

Make a list of the order in which you will do this.

If you have books in Select, do you plan to leave them there or move them wide and to your store? If so, do you have a timeframe? If not, write one.

TO DO

List all the products you will sell in your store.

RESOURCES

Book

The Mindful Entrepreneur: How to rapidly grow your business while staying sane, focused and fulfilled, Joel Gerschman, Howard Finger, Aryeh Goldman.

8. WHY SELL DIRECT? THE BENEFITS!

> Things that seem unimaginable today will seem inevitable tomorrow.

> — DUMBLEDORE, *FANTASTIC BEASTS: THE SECRETS OF DUMBLEDORE*

Why sell direct? The benefits!

You get the money immediately. You do not have to wait for up to 60 days. That takes care of cash flow problems!

You also won't have money deducted from your royalties. No more receiving 35%, 60%, or 70% of your book sales–you get 100%! Well, minus credit card fees, of course, but as authors, we really don't have many expenses other than production and marketing. We don't have to pay rent for a brick and mortar store, pay for a store fit-out, employ staff in high numbers, or commute to work.

One of the big benefits of selling direct is financial security. Even if you're not doing much with your store, if your retailer account were to be shut down, if a retailer suddenly had issues paying you, or if one of the retailers went bottoms-up, you would have a level of security. You could then focus your marketing attention on your store. At the very least, it's a good safety net.

Another benefit of selling direct is that your advertising dollar goes to you! This is particularly important once you take a wider view than an author-focused view of advertising.

I have noticed that authors are obsessed solely with ROI (Return on Investment) for their ads. This is far from industry standard. As an aside, I should add that the authors are actually focused on ROAS (Return on Ad Spend) but are calling it ROI.

ROI takes into account more than the ad spend. ROAS simply takes the ad spend into account.

An example of a ROAS ad is where you advertise a book and make $5 on each sale. The ad costs $100. You need to sell 20 books to cover your costs.

In advertising, there are various types of desired ad outcomes, only one type of which is ROAS. Authors often complain that they had to switch off their ads as they did not sell enough products to cover the cost of the ad.

Authors rarely mention any other type of ad, but ROAS is only one type of ad. Authors often do not realise the ads they have designated as ROAS also create brand awareness.

Think of the ads you see on TV. Are they all designed to sell a specific product? No. Okay, I just switched on the free-to-air TV to see what ads would be shown to me in the one segment.

Fluffy fleece jackets $15
Washers and dryers - a chain store's range
A vitamin range
A supermarket saying they do home delivery

The Body Shop "let's make real change" – not showing a single product.
An insurance company stating it helps the community – not mentioning any product.

What are the other types of ads? Companies have advertising strategies to increase brand awareness and not simply to gain direct revenue. The famous advertising guru, David Ogilvie, said, "Every advertisement is a long term investment in the image of a brand."

One strong method of advertising is to position the brand in the mind of the customer.

What is positioning? (A classic book on the subject is *Positioning, the Battle For Your* Mind by Ries and Trout.) Put simply, a brand is positioned against others. A famous example is that Avis did not become highly profitable until their ad which positioned them as Number 2 was released: "Avis is only Number 2 in rent-a-cars. So why go with us? We try harder."

For cozy mysteries, this might be having the words, "No intimate scenes, no gore, no swearing" in the ad. Saying what a product does not have can be effective–from the "horseless carriage" to "sugar free sodas."

Positioning is getting the reality of the brand across to the customer in a way which influences the customer's perception of the brand.

I digress a little. The main purpose of advertising should not simply be to sell a specific mentioned product at a profit. Sure, this can be part of your advertising strategy, but you do need a strategy that is more than ROAS. Part of that strategy should be brand strengthening and brand awareness.

When The Body Shop runs an ad saying they make real change, they are not advertising a single product. They are, however, demonstrating how they would like their brand to be perceived and creating awareness for their brand. From this, they gain customers, and customers buy.

An alternative would have been to run an ad for a vanilla-scented hand cream. See the difference! When you run an ad for your book and lament that the ad has not earned out, instead consider that your ad was promoting brand awareness. (I'm not saying to run ads all the time at a ROAS loss, either. I'm talking overall strategy here.)

Other objectives of advertising are to build brand image and awareness, to strengthen the brand, to gain newsletter subscribers, and to increase engagement on social media.

Advertising is not all about ROAS.

Amazon shows authors' ebook ads to paperback buyers. Why? In his book, *Amazon Ads Unleashed*, Robert J. Ryan noted that Amazon is happy to show authors' ebook ads on paperback titles. He explained that, in his opinion, Amazon is attempting to lure readers of traditionally published paperback books over to the Kindle store. He goes into this in some depth, stating that Amazon is using your advertising dollar to accomplish this. He also mentions that real estate agents often talk their clients into advertising in statewide publications. This does not help the home owner; rather, it increases brand awareness for the real estate business, again, using the home owner's advertising dollar.

The bottom line is that when an author runs an ad to a retailer, the author is generally hoping for ROAS alone. However, those ads, paid for by the author, are promoting that retailer's brand. The author's hard-earned money is paying to advertise the retailer itself.

When you sell direct, you can spend the bulk of your advertising budget on your own store. Your ad is promoting your own brand.

If you didn't want to go all-in with a store at this point, you could at least sell new releases in your store for a few weeks before launching on the retailers.

You can sell AI narrated audiobooks if you wish. At the time of writing, Audible will not accept digitally narrated audiobooks: your submitted audiobook must be narrated by a human.[1]

Another benefit of selling direct is that there won't be ads for other people's books on your books, and the customer won't be prompted to buy a book that's not yours.

Your retailer product page will have only your book or books on it. Think about it. When you run an Amazon ad, your book isn't the only product on that page. You are contributing to Amazon's bottom line.

With a store, you have customer data. You will know where your customers came from. You own the purchase data of your customers. If you run an email blast promotion or run ads, you will know precisely how many sales were referred from the promotion or ad.

You can get customers onto your newsletter list directly from your store. You can develop a relationship with readers. This will become increasingly important as AI becomes more mainstream. When AI narrated fiction books arrive—and they will!—authors who ride the tide better will be those who have developed a relationship with their readers.

Customers don't leave the platform and go somewhere else to buy your books.

You can reach countries that the major retailers don't reach.

You have control. Your store is not subject to the whims or caprice of the major retailers and some retailers' wayward bots.

You control the customer experience.

More benefits.

It's easier to deal with author spite and harassment tactics.

For a while, my Amazon Quality Issue Dashboard was filled daily with a high number of fake reported-by-reader issues, such as saying 'house' should be replaced with 'house' and so on. I had dozens of these on a daily basis.

Some time ago, every time I released a book that had been on preorder, I would receive a one star review on the book in both the UK and US from the same person within 15 minutes of it going live. It didn't matter if it was Book 10 in a series, and it was clear from the reviews that the reviewer hadn't read the book. I also received various alleged infringement notices from a retailer about the same book. Although these warnings were always sorted in my favour eventually, it cost me time and peace of mind.

Paid non-fiction newsletters are now popular. If you're a non-fiction author, you could sell a subscription for maybe $5 a week or a month. These are low-price, high volume, like ebooks!

Objections to selling direct.

You don't want to handle Support.

You don't want to spend time telling people how to get their files onto their ereader.

You don't have to! Many shopfronts handle delivery of digital files, but you could (should!) use a service such as BookFunnel to deliver ebook and audio files. I use BookFunnel as it also handles support.

You don't want to pay for print books in advance, handle stock, and run to the post office. And what if you wanted a nice week away at the beach?

Fair enough! Go and have a week away at the beach. It sounds like fun! (Although as an Aussie, I associate beaches with sharks. I like sharks, but I also stay on dry land.) You can sell print books from your store without ever touching the books, let alone shipping them.

The solution is easy. If you have either Shopify or WooCommerce, you can integrate with BookVault or Lulu Direct (used to be known as Lulu xPress).

All you do is set up the product page in Shopify or WooCommerce and set up the files in BookVault or Lulu Direct. It's super easy and fast, and after the initial set-up, you don't have to do a thing. (Disclaimer: if you have over 100 books, it will be a drag uploading all those books. Short term pain, long term gain! Try to ignore the RSI and shoulder pain!)

This is how it works. The fictional customer, Mary Smith, buys a print book from your Shopify or WooCommerce store. The store automatically deposits the money into your account. Your store automatically notifies BookVault or Lulu Direct. Lulu Direct takes their share of money from your account. With BookVault, you put some money (from £10 - around $12 USD - to whatever you wish) in your BookVault account first. BookVault emails you when you need to top up. BookVault or Lulu Direct prints and ships the book direct to Mary Smith.

If you live in the US or Canada and don't want to use Shopify or WooCommerce, you could use Aerio. Aerio is Ingram's customer direct selling tool. However Aerio, unlike BookVault and Lulu Direct, does not ship internationally and is location restricted.

To set up an Aerio account, you simply need your books set up in IngramSpark and available for distribution. Ingram prints and ships all orders. There are alternatives: skip to the chapter on selling print.

What about my Amazon rankings?

Some authors point out you won't get the rankings on the retailers when you have already sold numerous copies in your store. Those of us who are wide are used to not so great rankings on Amazon anyway, given that a borrow counts as a sale for ranking purposes. A book selling wide can never rank anywhere near as well as it would have had it been in Kindle Select.

Consider this: would you rather have direct customers or Amazon's customers?

When you first open a store, you won't have enough sales to impact the Amazon rank to any significant degree. By the time you do, you won't care.

Sure, high rankings help organic sales, but if you're wide, you are positioned far behind all the Select authors anyway. It's worth repeating that for Amazon rankings, a borrow counts as a sale. Your book which sold for maybe $4.99 is ranked the same as a borrow with maybe a single 0.0045c page read. An author friend of mine had a newish release of her German translation in Germany making around $30 a day and ranking around 15,000 to 20,000. She put it in Kindle Select, and the book at once ranked around 1,500 and stayed there for some time. She was still making just over $30 a day.

If you're worried that your store sales will cannibalise your Amazon sales, consider: you can do so much more when you have the data of your customers. If you go about things the right way, you can make more from your store than you made on any one retailer.

A retailer isn't pushing books to your store.

That's true! Yet consider this: when was the last time a retailer pushed one of your books (for free, that is)?

Sure, a high Amazon ranking will push organic sales of your book, but with a store, you have plenty of ways to attract, keep, cross sell and upsell customers. Don't think of Amazon as the *norm* and a store as the *other*. Selling direct requires a mindset shift. Your store is not just another retailer.

It won't work for my genre.

How many times have I heard this over the years? For years, I've been making 6 figures a year wide with my paranormal cozy mysteries, and for years, people have been saying paranormal cozy mysteries won't sell outside Kindle Unlimited.

People run with these narratives which are simply logical fallacies; people assume they're true because others agree with them.

If it sells somewhere, it will sell somewhere else. You simply need a sound strategy.

Tax is a nightmare!

Isn't it always? Who likes tax? Nobody, really. It's no fun at all.

When we sell direct, we need to be aware of sales tax.

Authors typically throw up their hands in horror at the thought of sales tax, but think on this: every single ecommerce business deals with sales tax. If they can do it, so can you.

Disclaimer! I'm not a sales tax agent or a sales tax account. I'm mathematically challenged, and spreadsheets frighten me almost as much as venomous snakes. (There are plenty of such snakes in Australia. Probably more than spread-sheets.) So what I say about sales tax is not professional advice and is what I have discovered as somebody who pays sales tax. Please consult a professional or get a sales tax app. This is not advice but rather, my experience.

Just to make things difficult, there are different laws for different US states. It's all location, location, location.

Sales tax is paid depending on the location of the buyer, with a caveat.

However, there are other laws dependent upon where you as the seller live, and whether you have a physical sales presence such as a warehouse or office in the US. There are also various tax laws for the UK and EU, and these differ as to whether the products are digital, whether those digital products are ebooks or audiobooks, and whether you are selling to a customer or to another business.

If you sell to Australia, you need to hit $75,000 AUD in 12 months just from sales to Australia before you need to collect sales tax from Australians.

If you live in the US, you will have physical nexus (think of nexus as the point when somebody needs to collect and pay sales tax from their customers) depending on your state, and every state has different laws. Some US states, Alaska, Delaware, Montana, New Hampshire and Oregon, do not have any sales tax (yay!) and others have no sales tax on digital goods.

Economic nexus (where the buyer lives; the seller could be on Mars) depends on the US state, and this varies from zero to $500,000 in 1 year (or 200 transactions in 1 year) depending on the US state. Once you reach economic nexus, you need to file and remit taxes. Still, I'm sure the blow would be softened if you made $500,000 in print books in 12 months in California, for example.

Some sales tax apps/plugins collect and remit tax; some don't. In great news, Shopify has introduced Shopify Tax (for the US for now, but it will expand) which calculates US tax for you. It won't remit it, but it does calculate it.

EU tax, however, is a different matter.

You don't have to figure it out for yourself or waste any time on it. Storefronts such as Shopify and WooCommerce will tell you if and when you have a tax liability, as will apps/plugins. Some apps/plugins do 100% of the work and figure it out automatically, file, and pay. I should mention that Lulu Direct collects and pays sales tax on print books. Payhip handles digital goods sales tax for the UK and EU.

So then, sales tax isn't as bad as it sounds! It's just the thought of it that's downright unpleasant. I go into more detail about sales tax in a later chapter. And I do have a course on International sales tax for those who want it all made easy.

.

RESOURCES

QUESTIONS

In your view, what are the major benefits of selling direct?

List your objections to selling direct. Are any of these objections due to the author-selling-on-retailers mindset?

RESOURCES

Books

Tools Of Titans: The Tactics, Routines, and Habits of Billionaires, Icons, and World-Class Performers, Timothy Ferriss

The 80/20 Principle: The Secret to Achieving More with Less, Richard Koch

9. THE BOOK WHISPERER

> 66 The trouble with the world is not that
> people know too little; it's that they
> know so many things that just aren't so.

— MARK TWAIN

There's a common (mis)conception that it's
difficult to train readers to buy from your store.

Do you need to train readers to buy from you?

No, not really. It's a matter of visibility rather than
persuasion. For readers to buy from your store,
they need to know you have a store.

The other day I wanted to buy coats for my dogs.
We'd had a cold snap, and my rescue Dingo

doesn't like the cold at all. (My chocolate Labrador only thinks about food, not the weather.) I looked online. I found the same suitable dog coat on several different stores, and then I was pleased to find the manufacturer of the coats sold direct from their website. I inherently trusted this site more, and that's where I bought the dog coat. Am I alone in this thinking? No.

Selling direct to the consumer (DTC or D2C) has been commonplace for most non-author businesses for some time, with businesses switching from the old traditional retail sales model. Many big brands have done away with the "middleman." By bypassing retailers, businesses have taken control of their brand, their customers, their messaging, their data, and their analytics. And you can too!

It's difficult to establish and maintain a good relationship with customers when you are selling through retailers. If you sell through a retailer, you cannot collect data such as customer experience. You cannot analyse customer buying behaviour, and you cannot understand customer purchase decisions.

So, how do you become visible?

One simple, and better still, free, way to do this is to link to your store in the back matter and/or where you mention the next book in the series (assuming you write in series, that is). You could do this directly in your backmatter (as I do—I only link to my store) or have a link to your website on which you have a link to your store followed by a link to the retailers. That way, you are using the retailer to gain customers instead of the retailer using you to gain customers.

Let the retailers work for you instead of you working for the retailers.

And don't neglect ads to the retailers. I myself don't make Amazon ads a priority, but the major retailers are a wonderful source of customers for your store when you are starting out selling direct. If you are familiar with Dean Wesley Smith's *The Magic Bakery* concept, the major retailers are a huge open door to your bakery. As a caveat, if you are advertising a first in series free, the readthrough from the other main retailers, Barnes & Noble, Kobo, GooglePlay, and Apple, is far better than the readthrough from Amazon.

Tell your newsletter list about your store. Rather than simply telling your list that you have a store, give them a link to a product. (Offering too wide a choice can be counterproductive. It's called Buyer Paralysis.)

You can advertise directly to products (yes, books are products!) in your store on Facebook or BookBub (BookBub ads, that is, not Featured Deals). You can run ads to your ebooks and audio-books in BookBub ads.

A BookBub Featured Deal is a good way to drive customers to your store, despite the fact you cannot link directly to your store with a Deal. Advertise a first-in-series for free or at 99c, and then in your back matter, link the next book in the series to your store. (Don't use free in your store itself.)

If you have a Shopify or WooCommerce store, you can integrate with Pinterest, Facebook, Instagram, TikTok, and/or Google, and sell your products there for free. However, Facebook and Instagram will not accept digital content. (Some might slip through from time to time.) Google Shopping will not accept digital products.

You can integrate Shopify with your Pinterest business account, and then every pin from your store is a Shoppable Pin. At the time of writing, Pinterest gives a $100 USD advertising credit to all sellers integrating their Pinterest accounts with Shopify.

You could put up a preorder in your store alone before putting it on the major retailers.

The basics which were important when you sold solely to retailers are still important, only you might look at them differently now. There are fewer limitations. Maybe you will add Google ads or YouTube ads, even influencer marketing, to your repertoire. Having a store is the time to think outside the proverbial box.

Now, reviews are easier to obtain. Simply add a review app/plugin to your store, set it to your liking, and let the app collect reviews and place them on your product page. The app will even remind readers to request reviews if you set it to do so. You can set and forget.

As more authors sell direct, more customers will search for author stores. People are already used to buying non-book items online. Shopify alone has well over 2 million daily active users.

In KDP Select? Not a problem. You can put audiobooks and print books in your store, and any

ebooks not in Select, as well as preorder ebooks
(and wait until release to put them in Select).

RESOURCES

QUESTIONS

What ways can you get customers to your store?

Have you told your newsletter list about your store?

RESOURCES

Books

The Magic Bakery - Dean Wesley Smith

Foundr Version 1.0: The Ultimate Startup Manual: Everything you need to know about starting and building a successful business, from the world's most influential entre-preneurs, Foundr Media.

Podcast

How I Built This npr.org/series/490248027/how-i-built-this

10. INFLUENCER MARKETING

> " People do not buy goods and services.
> They buy relations, stories, and magic.

— SETH GODIN

As authors, we are used to email marketing and not much else. Ecommerce sellers also use SMS marketing and influencer marketing. Again, this is easier for non-fiction authors.

People often think of celebrities when they hear the word "influencer," but celebrities are generally considered the worst form of influencer marketing. This once was not the case, but social media changes rapidly. Being an influencer is about relationships and communication, so influencers with fewer followers often prove the best form of marketing.

The influencer marketing industry is worth around $14 billion. A survey published by the Influencer Marketing Hub on March 29th, 2022, found that businesses make $5.20 for every dollar they spend on influencer marketing.

With influencer marketing, you get exposure and endorsements from influencers from TikTok (which has the highest engagement rate), Instagram, and YouTube, even Facebook, Twitter, and Twitch.

The challenge is to find influencers who will suit your brand—and it can be difficult to find ones who suit genre fiction books in general!

The usual methods are to give products to the influencer, to pay for a sponsored endorsement, to give the influencer a cut of profits, or to collaborate on an influencer's post. The latter is less usual for books. Some give a discount code for the influencer to give people. This makes sales easy to track.

Start small with influencers until you learn the ropes. Make sure your Instagram feed reflects your branding and isn't a hot mess with incongruent content, as influencers won't want to work with content like that.

You can contact the influencer directly or via what was once Dovetale, acquired as an app by Shopify in early 2022 and in August 2022 embedded in Shopify admin as Shopify Collabs. Shopify Collabs is accessed after installing the free app. This enables you to create an application page as well as manage affiliate payouts should you decide to go that way. No doubt Shopify Collabs will keep evolving.

Collabs only allows you to offer free products or a discount code (percentage or dollar). It does not allow you to offer monetary payment as such, but watch for the autopopulated list that appears under Perks. You can remove some of the suggested perks, but you can add another form of compensation next to an icon, which happily is a dollar sign. I wrote, "At influencer request."

Perks

☆ Get featured

🎁 Product giveaways

🏷 Discount codes

♡ Collab opportunities

$ At influencer request

It also prompts you to fill out your profile, which you can customise. Shopify Collabs only accepts PayPal as the payment method. With Collabs, you can search hashtags and view stats such as engagement rates for influencers. However, you cannot contact an influencer, but you can see their social media handles, and sometimes the influencer will provide their email.

Instead of Shopify Collabs, you can use Shoutcart. (Shoutcart is not an app and is nothing to do with Shopify or any selling platform.) With Shoutcart, anybody can buy a shoutout simply by adding it to their cart. Shoutcart also provides stats on influencers such as cost, engagement, and ROI. It can be hard to find keyword results for genre fiction on Shoutcart, but it's a simple process. The free plan currently allows you to unlock contact information on three influencers.

With Shoutcart, so you don't waste your three unlocks, I suggest tracking down the influencer with the scant information Shoutcart provides, namely, part of a social media handle and an ambiguous sentence or two. For example, I searched "ecommerce" and after some time found the influencers, but they were involved in real estate. Had I not looked for the influencers on social media first, I would have wasted my unlocks.

Other influencer platforms are Whalar, Influence.co, Grin, Upfluence, Klear, TapInfluence, Inlfuencity, and Grapevine.

Influencers fall into 5 categories:

1. Nano influencer - less than 10,000 followers. (Some define a nano influencer as having less than 5,000 followers.)

Nano influencers topically change between $30 and $300 for a social media post. Specifically, expect to pay around $30 for a Facebook post and around $100 for an Instagram post.

Yes, it's counterintuitive to select influencers with this small number of followers, but their followers are typically highly engaged and don't expect the influencers to sell to them. The downside is that Nano influencers might have scant experience. Still, surveys have shown that those with less than 5,000 followers have the highest engagement rate.

2. Micro influencers - 5,000 - 20,000 followers.

(Yes, some define Micro influencers as having 10,000 -20,000 followers.)

47.3% of influencers are Micro influencers. Expect to pay around $300 for a Facebook post and around $170 for an Instagram post.

3. Mid tier influencers - 10,000 to 100,000 followers.

(Again, some define Mid tier influencers as having 20,000 -20,000 followers.)

These usually get a good (and fast) return on investment but typically command high prices for their services.

The downside is that the audience might not be engaged. Typically, the higher the number of followers, the more likely the influencers have followers in countries where you don't have a market.

4. Mega influencers - between 100,000 and 1 million followers.

5. Celebrity influencers - over 1 million followers.

If you wish to contact an influencer directly, introduce yourself, and make it clear that you know something about them. Do your research! Make it clear you are familiar with their brand. If they are vegan for example, don't ask them to endorse a book about leather work. Tell them what you want. Keep it fairly short and to the point, and include your social media handles. Do not offer them a free book in return. They will want a lot more than that!

It's also a good idea to engage on the influencer's platform for some time before you approach them.

It's acceptable to ask for their analytics to ascertain if they are a good fit. It's also acceptable (and advisable!) to ask for their rates.

When the influencer agrees, tell them the points of your book or product you would like them to mention. Don't go over the top! If you give the influencer too many points, their mention of your book/product won't sound natural or organic, and that will defeat the purpose.

No doubt you have heard of bookstagram and booktok. Finding bookstagrammer influencer marketers is not easy. Search for these hashtags on Instagram.

#bookstagram #instabook #bookphotography #bookstagrammer #readersofinstagram #booklover #bookworm #bookish #books #booknerd #book #bibliophile #bookaddict #bookaddiction #reading #amreading #booka-holic #booksofinstagram #ilovereading

#booklover #bookhaul #booklove #bookhoarder #booknerds #fortheloveofbooks #instabook #bookblog #igreads #igbooks #bookshelf #book-shelves #bookworm #bookreview #booksbooks-books #reader #bookcommunity #bookobsessed #bookblogger #read #ilovebooks #bookstoread #bookreview #bookpics #bookrecs #bookblog

Search for these hashtags on Booktok.

#booktok #booktoker #bookworm #bookrecs #writing #book #books #booknerd #bookclub #bookish #reader #bookreview #booklover #bookobsessed #bookofthemonth #bookclub #bookrecommendations #whatareyoureading #read #reading #booklove

Also search for hashtags associated with your genre.

RESOURCES

QUESTIONS

What hashtags suit your genre on:

1. Instagram

2. TikTok?

Can you think of non-book influencers you could approach?

RESOURCES

Books

Winfluence: Reframing Influencer Marketing to Ignite Your Brand, Jason Falls

The Influencer Code: How to Unlock the Power of Influencer Marketing, Amanda Russell, Jesse Itzler

11. EMAIL AND SMS MARKETING

> Mobile is not the future, it is the now. Meet your customers in the environment of their choice, not where it's convenient for you.

— CYNDIE SHAFFSTALL, SOFTWARE ENTREPRENEUR, FOUNDER OF SPIDER TRAINERS

As authors, we are used to email marketing, but ecommerce and mobile commerce businesses make great use of SMS marketing. SMS marketing has 4 times the click rate and 23 times the conversion rate of email marketing.

Authors selling on retailers use lead magnets, but ecommerce businesses use offers. Typically, the welcome email at the end of the flow includes an offer. An offer is typically a discount (10%, 15%, 20%, sometimes even 25%) or other attractive offer.

Remember to put your discount code on the confirmation page.

Which email service provider to use?

The good old email service providers used by authors are often limited for ecommerce. On the other hand, ecommerce email service providers will integrate seamlessly with your store—depending on your store—and you will easily be able to segment. With minimal effort on your part, you can segment customers who have not bought anything in a certain time frame, as well as customers who have bought only in one series. You will have a segment of VIPs, customers who have bought over a certain dollar amount (which you set).

Segments allow you to cross sell to customers who have purchased in one series but not in another, for example.

Instead of migrating your list from your old email service provider to your ecommerce email service provider, you can simply keep both running. As your old list organically moves to your store list (by means of subscribers purchasing from your store), you can delete those subscribers from your old list. That keeps your new list nice and clean and has subscribers who are buyers-on-store rather than buyers-on-retailers. Otherwise, you would most likely have drop-off rates. Sure, it's a bit of work, but business does require effort. You'll be happy in the long run!

Examples of ecommerce email service provider apps are Klaviyo, Omnisend, and Privy. These apps do SMS marketing as well, but some businesses add the Postscript app or the SMS Bump app, and these two apps are SMS-only marketing.

Tip.

Be aware that platforms can call the same thing different names. For example, Active Campaign (in automation triggers) uses "product" and Shopify uses "type" to refer to the very same thing.

Pop-up.

The author-selling-on-retailers way to collect subscribers is to have a sign-up form in the front or back of your books. The author-selling-on-store way is to have a pop-up form.

Your pop-up form can include an offer such as a discount code (recommended!), or it can simply be a pop-up form (not recommended).

Research has shown that a dual pop-up form (email then SMS, plus an offer) has a better conversion rate than any other form, whether email only or a form with both email and SMS fields. Yes, that does sound counter-intuitive, but that's the way it is. Strange but true!

Don't have the pop-up set to, well, pop up (!) as soon as somebody opens the site. Go to your analytics and find out the average session time for your store. See how long it takes for a customer to leave your store, and set the pop-up to 5 seconds before that. That way you are not annoying the customer with an in-your-face pop-up before they've had a chance to look around a little.

Double opt-in.

Yes, you need to have a double opt-in. The exception here is if you have a 1-tap SMS-only pop-up for mobile devices, as these collect the phone numbers automatically.

Double opt-ins improve your sender reputation and email deliverability.

Unsubscribe link.

Authors know to place a clear unsubscribe link in the footer of an email. It's a good idea to add your contact email as well.

FLOWS

Welcome automations/flows.

Authors selling on retailers generally use welcome automations/flows/sequences. (Automations, flows, sequences: same thing, different words.)

Welcome automations are also used in ecommerce. In the case of ecommerce, the first email arrives soon after purchase, while the customer is happy about their new purchase and the store is fresh in the customer's mind.

What is your email objective? Once you figure this out, you will know what content to send. You can use welcome emails to build trust, to show social proof, to educate customers about your books, to get customers to buy, or to tell them about yourself and your brand.

You can also survey customers to discover their preferences and buying habits.

It's a good idea to A/B test your welcome emails. Sometimes a little tweak can make a significant difference in income. You don't need to rush into this though. Take some time to become familiar with the system first.

It's worth repeating: it's best to send the first welcome email soon after someone subscribes, while your store is fresh in the customer's mind.

It might take some experimentation to set the timing of your subsequent emails. You don't want to overdo it by sending subsequent emails too soon, but you don't want to do it too late either or the customer will lose touch. You can split test the timing as well in Klaviyo.

Authors are usually savvy with the does and do-nots of welcome flows. Authors know to use personalisation, to avoid too many exclamation marks/points (we call them marks in Australia, by the way), to avoid too many emojis, to avoid too many links and images, and to avoid subject-line words that trigger spam filters. Of course, addressing somebody as "friend" or "dear" will send the email straight to spam.

Avoid fancy fonts and all capitals in emails as those can adversely affect deliverability rates.

Here are some words to avoid in subject lines:

Free, free gift, bargain, discount, cheap, lowest price, no cost, great offer, price, save, why pay more?, here, success, member, open, visit my/our website, 100% free, deal, giving away, unlimited, winner, compare, amazing, congratulations, act now, for you, limited time, offer expires, bonus.

The subject line should be designed to increase open rates. And remember to write something in the preview text section! Don't leave that blank. Surveys have found that optimised preview text can increase the open rate by 30 to 45%.

A welcome email with a conversational tone is advisable. You don't want to sound like a business manager. Be personable.

While I think of it, your Sender email address must be linked to your domain. Whatever you do, do not send it from your gmail address. It could be (your name)@(your domain).com, but it needs to be (something/anything!)@(your domain).com.

Use your brand colours in the email, but keep your fonts plain.

Abandoned checkout flow.

The objective of an abandoned checkout flow is to convert would-be customers into customers. You can customise it based on the items in the abandoned cart. You can also customise it based on whether they're already a customer.

As we sell books which are low cost items, we can send the first abandoned checkout email 15 minutes after the checkout is abandoned. The more highly priced the item, the longer you would leave the first email. I'll explain. If you have abandoned your checkout while buying a designer purse or an expensive retro refrigerator, you will need to think about it for a while—if you have abandoned your cart while buying a $14 paperback, not so much. It's easy to A/B test the time frame. I ran a split test with 15 minutes and 4 hours, and had the best conversion rates with 15 minutes.

Abandoned cart flow.

This should not be confused with the abandoned checkout flow. The cart is abandoned before the customer has entered their checkout information.

Again, as authors have lower-priced items, the time delays for the abandoned cart flow can be shorter.

Post Purchase flow.

These are also known as Thank You flows.

The post purchase flow is another important flow.

If a customer has bought a book in a series, you can send emails prompting the customer to buy the next book in the series, or better still, the next few books in the series.

This is also a good opportunity to survey your customers.

This flow can be split into first time buyers and previous buyers.

Winback flow.

This is for customers who have purchased at some point but have not bought again for some time. You can customise the email based on the products they've purchased and/or on the number of purchases they've made.

Browse abandonment flow.

Customers will receive messages based on the items they have looked at in your store. Browse abandonment flows remind customers what they were looking at even if they didn't put it in the cart.

There are other flows as well.

SMS MARKETING.

The compliance rules for SMS marketing are far stricter than email marketing rules. You must get explicit content from the subscriber to market to them by SMS. Having an already checked box saying something like "I consent to SMS marketing" does not cut it. That is not considered explicit consent.

You could send an email to your buying-on-retailer email list offering them a discount code to subscribe to your SMS marketing. The easier way to do this is simply to send them to your store and tell them to watch for the SMS pop-up. That way, you can transfer your customers from your old-school mailing list to your ecommerce list. (Remember to delete those customers from your old mailing list!)

SMS subscribers are considered more valuable than email subscribers.

RESOURCES

QUESTIONS

Which email service provider will you use for your store?

What flows will you set up in your store? Make a list.

What are the benefits of SMS marketing?

RESOURCES

Book

The Ecommerce Email Marketing Playbook: 80/20 Guide For Ecommerce Business Owners, Adam Moody

12. SEO

> The best place to hide a dead body is on the second page of Google search.

> — ANONYMOUS

SEO is highly important when you have your own author store.

What is SEO?

SEO is search engine optimisation. It's the process of improving the quality and quantity of website traffic to increase its visibility when people search for products or services related to your business.

The bottom line: with good SEO, you rank higher in search engines.

Before I get into it, when I say "Google" in this chapter (unless referring specifically to Google), I mean search engines in general. Another search engine is Bing. When I started out selling direct from websites 20 years ago, I bought software—it was a CD! It's probably in a museum now, along with floppy disks—that would index my sites to dozens of search engines. These days, there are barely any search engines.

Back in the day, people used to try SEO hacks such as putting keywords in white (or background-colour-matching) font so they were invisible to the naked eye but visible to spiders. Did I do that? Not fessing up! Oh, and a spider isn't a redback or a funnel-web spider, but a web crawling bot used for indexing.

SEO targets unpaid traffic, which means ads and social media are not included. Search engines see reviews as organic traffic, and so reviews contribute nicely to your product page's SEO. This leads to a higher SEO ranking for your store.

That reminds me—have you claimed your Knowledge Panel yet? Google yourself, and look for the panel on the right side of the search listing page. There will be a panel with your image and books below your image. At the bottom of the panel, you will see the words, "Claim this knowledge panel." Click on that and follow the prompts.

Google sees reviews as fresh content in a store and frequently, updated metadata ranks well. This content is usually keyword rich, so your store will rank higher for those keywords. In fact, Google loves reviews; it likes to see interaction with your site. Most review widgets are built to allow Google to crawl data such as images, text, and dates. Content stored in a page's HTML is easy for search engines to crawl.

Google also loves blogs, so you could link a blog to your store.

Slow loading sites increase bounce rate and lower conversion, and that's not good news for SEO.

With Shopify, you can optimise your content for SEO. You can edit the title tags, meta descriptions, and URLs for webpages, products, and collections —and blog posts if you have a blog. You should also edit the alt text for images.

No matter which storefront you use, make sure you add relevant keywords to your content, including page titles, descriptions, and image alt text. Search engines can't read images, but they can read alt text. Make sure you have used relevant keywords in the alt text for each image in your store.

Check your meta descriptions—are they keyword rich (without keyword spamming)? Before you upload your image files to your store, rename them with keywords describing the image. Therefore, instead of uploading an image with a file name such as "Thereallycorrectversionthis-timex9," name it "Dragonsciencefiction" or whatever suits your genre.

If you link to other parts of your store, describe the text to which you're linking. So then, if you have the words, "Check out my great new Urban Fantasy," link the words "Urban Fantasy" rather than the entire sentence. Don't say, "Check out my great new Urban Fantasy here," and link the word "here.'

What makes your site rank higher?

1. Links pointing to your store from other sites. These links do not include paid links (such as from ads) or social media links.

2. The age of your domain name.

3. Engagement on your site.

4. Content and website structure optimised for search engines. That is, the search engines see your content as relevant to your products.

5. Verify your store with Google, and link your sitemap to Google. (Your sitemap is every page on your site.) To do this, go to Google Search Console and follow the prompts.

6. Fast-loading sites/stores! This is a big one. Read on!

RESOURCES

QUESTIONS

Have you claimed your Knowledge Panel?

Are your meta descriptions keyword rich?

Have you named your image files with keywords describing the image?

Have you named your image alt text?

Have you verified your store with Google and linked your sitemap to Google?

RESOURCES

How to claim your knowledge panel on Google. Copy the below.

http://support.google.com/knowledgepanel/answer/753490

2?hl=en

13. IMPROVING STORE SPEED

66 A 2-second delay in load time resulted in abandonment rates of up to 87%.

— DOUBLECLICK (OWNED BY GOOGLE) SEPTEMBER 2016 BY *ALEX SHELLHAMMER*

66 If your plans don't include mobile, your plans are not finished.

— WENDY CLARK, FORMER SVP AT COCA-COLA

Mobile commerce is bigger than ecommerce, and so it's more important than ever that your store/website is optimised for mobile devices. This means the page looks one way on a laptop/desktop and another way (a good way!) on a mobile device. The page and the site itself must be easy for the customer to navigate.

Have you ever gone to a website on a mobile device and couldn't make head or tail of it? Was one side of it missing? Did it take ages to load? Remember how irritated you were and all the rude words you muttered? Or maybe you're not like I am—maybe you're all calm and Zen. Still, people do expect a site to look good and to be easy to navigate on a mobile device. Customers vote with their feet.

In 2014, Emma Crowe, Senior Vice President of Client Strategy at Somo, stated, "The adoption rate of mobile is twice that of the internet, three times that of social media, and 10 times faster than PCs."

Increasingly, consumers rely on their smartphones and tablets for purchases. I'm a cozy mystery author, and my demographic is women over 65, but in my store, two-thirds of my customers buy on mobile devices. As direct sellers, we need to know how and where our customers buy.

It's super important to have a fast-landing store or customers will leave. According to Google, 53% of visits are abandoned if a site takes longer than 3 seconds to load.[1] However, most ecommerce mobile sites take around 6.9 seconds to load, so more than half the visitors have fled by then taking their money with them, money the seller could have had.

It's no surprise that Google ranks faster-loading stores higher. With faster mobile page speed and improved SEO, your site will appear in top search carousels and what's more, earn a lower Cost Per Click on Google Ads.

That's a reason not to have too many apps/plug-ins, as many of them slow down your store. If you delete an app, it's a good idea to delete any code the app left behind.

Many customers buy on mobile devices, and so it's vital to optimise your store for mobile devices.

RESOURCES

QUESTIONS

How does your store (or website) look on a mobile
device?

RESOURCES

YouTube

How To Do SEO And Optimize Your Online
Store For The Search Engines, MyWifeQuit-
HerJob Ecommerce Channel

youtube.com/watch?v=7EV36uQbN1E

14. APPS AND PLUGINS

> An investment in knowledge pays the
> best interest.

— BENJAMIN FRANKLIN

Don't go crazy adding apps. Every app you use
will likely slow down your store to some degree,
and what's more, non-free apps add to your
running costs!

Having said that, let's look at some apps (called
plugins on WooCommerce) which could prove
useful to your store.

Before I forget, most apps don't require you to add
code to your website, thank goodness. You just
download the app, and Bob's your uncle! So when

selecting an app, make sure it's a one-click install rather than a "We need you to add a piece of simple code to your store" install. (Not everybody has the same definition of simple.)

As booksellers, our products are low-price, high-volume.

It's a challenge, as is the fact that most ecommerce advice out there is for dropshippers.

Low-price, high-volume becomes a pitfall when dealing with Shopify or WooCommerce and some apps/plugins, as the price point of several apps depends on your number of monthly orders. It's easy for an author to have a high number of monthly sales but quite a low value of turnover, whereas the apps are assuming a far higher $ turnover. The nature of our industry makes these apps costly.

Apps generally are geared to the most popular industries, such as clothing. There are over 1.75 million Shopify stores, and of those, over 750,500 sell clothing. You won't get a pair of jeans online for $4.99. When choosing apps, be wary of ones that charge by the number of monthly orders.

I give examples of apps below, but it doesn't mean I recommend them. (And I haven't tried them all.)

BOOKFUNNEL.

Not an app but will save your sanity. Seriously!

BookFunnel delivers ebook files and audio files. It integrates seamlessly with Shopify, WooCommerce, PayPal, and Payhip.

I consider BookFunnel to be a must-have. Sure, you might have a store that delivers digital files, but what about support? Do you want to wake up to emails from a customer saying he entered his password for his library, and it looked like a line of asterisks?

And here's another thing: customers can save their books in their BookFunnel library. Those books will be nice and safe. I've heard of all sorts of disasters where readers have stored their ebooks on specific-to-retailer devices. You've no doubt heard of bots shutting down author accounts? Bots are also shutting down some customer accounts at said retailers. Readers report they lose all ebooks stored on their specific-to-retailer devices along with their account. On the other hand, BookFunnel will store a reader's books in complete safety.

. . .

BOOKVAULT, LULU DIRECT (or alternative).

These are third party apps that print and ship your books globally, usually with local shipping rates. Go to the chapter on Selling Print.

A REVIEW APP.

A review app is great. It will email customers and ask them to leave a review. The process is made as easy as possible for the customer.

Review apps provide your store with social proof and also enhance your SEO.

Check the number of monthly reviews each plan allocates.

There's a little catch for fiction authors—some review apps block reviews with words such as murder, corpse, poison, death. I found this out the hard way! Never mind, you will be able to whitelist these words.

Also, make sure your review app doesn't collect site reviews as well. You want product reviews. If it collects both, turn off the site reviews. Stay on top of this too. If a reviewer app's support insists something has been fixed, check for yourself. (Yes, I'm speaking from experience. Shaking head and sighing.)

You can also set up your review app to post automatically for 4 stars and above. Anything else, you moderate. This is a good safety valve if you have a mad relative who leaves vitriol on all your products. Ex-partner, anybody? You know what I mean.

Having said that, make sure you do let the unfavourable yet honest reviews about the book through. Still, I've found that people tend not to dislike the books of an author from whom they have bought direct.

Don't be tempted to let the review app import reviews from Amazon or the like. The reviewer owns the copyright. You cannot repost reviews from Amazon or another retailer site without the reviewers' express permission. Well, you can, but you should not,, as it's a breach of copyright. The bigger review apps don't offer this option, at any rate.

If you start with one review app and don't like it, it is generally easy to migrate those reviews to another review app. Check if this is possible before adding the new review app. If you can't figure out how to do it, the review app's support people will usually do it for you with no extra cost involved.

I use and recommend Loox.

Examples:

Shopify: Loox, Okendo, Yotpo, JudgeMe, Review-Nudge, Fera, Stamped.io.

WooCommerce: Yotpo, Product Reviews Pro, Stamped.io, JudgeMe.

A FREQUENTLY BOUGHT TOGETHER APP.

A Frequently Bought Together app will automatically recommend related products to your customers based on the current product they are looking at and their purchase history.

This one app will do wonders for increasing your conversion rates. You will see this same type of system on Amazon product pages.

Shopify: The Frequently Bought Together app plus various upsell and cross sell apps.

WooCommerce: The Frequently Bought Together app plus various upsell and cross sell apps.

BUNDLE, UPSELL, POST SELL, CROSS-SELL APPS.

A Bundle app works in a similar way to a Frequently Bought Together app, but you can offer a discount.

Remember the words, "Do you want fries with that?" That's an upsell! And upsells have huge money-making potential.

Brick and mortar stores have products near checkout to encourage impulse buying. This is a proven strategy.

These usually all-in-one apps increase the average order value by offering at least one other product. Most offer a one-click purchase offer. These apps tend to convert well. Some offer shopping cart pop-up discounts. Some will collect customers' birthdays so you can send out a birthday offer/discount.

With a post sell app on a thank you page, customers can accept a post-purchase offer in one click, without the need to re-enter payment information or check out again. Most offer countdown timers. The cost of acquiring this customer is zero, and the open rate for that page is 100%.

For example, I use Klaviyo for email and SMS marketing, and I also use the Reconvert Upsell & Cross sell app. I have integrated the two. I also have an option to collect birthdays on the thank you page to collect emails so I can send each customer who has filled in their birthdate a discount on their birthday. Reconvert collects the birthdays and instantly sends them to Klaviyo which instantly segments the customers for their birthdays. It might sound complicated, but it's not. I give instructions for this in my selling direct course.

Examples:

Shopify: Reconvert Upsell & Cross sell, Upsell Plus Checkout Upsell, Bold Upsell, candy Cart, AfterSell Post Purchase Upsell, and Salesboost Upsell & Cross Sell.

WooCommerce: Checkout X, One Click Upsell Funnel, Product Bundles, Checkout Add-Ons.

EMAIL SERVICE PROVIDER APP.

You're probably not thinking of an email service provider as an app, but we're talking ecommerce! The Klaviyo app is amazing and beyond easy to use. Ever turned to day drinking when trying to set up an automation flow? Turn to Klaviyo instead. Your liver will thank you.

I've been with Mad Mimi, Mailchimp, MailerLite, and ActiveCampaign—and another one I will not name, one which seemed to assign special known-only-to-them word meanings to common words, had numerous different departments none of which spoke to each other, and when they become angry, would send emails in bold explaining the special word meanings they used only in their company. Strangely, unsubscribing from them repeatedly did not work. Dealing with them was like being in a Monty Python movie, only not funny.

If you want a serious business, in my honest opin-ion, Klaviyo leaves all others for dead. What's more, Klaviyo has amazing templates. Yes, I hear you say, so do most email service providers. But not like Klaviyo's templates! These are user-friendly on steroids.

Klaviyo is a dedicated ecommerce setup and can do SMS marketing as well as email marketing.

Setting it up is so easy (that is, if you've ever used an email service provider before) you won't even need comfort food!

With Klaviyo, you can do all sorts of clever things without much effort. You can easily segment your lists by product purchase, for example. Write in different genres? No worries! It's simple to segment buyers by purchase type.

Klaviyo collects all your customer data and provides a way to act on it.

Klaviyo will import your store theme for your branding.

Klaviyo integrates with Shopify, WooCommerce, BigCommerce, and Magento.

AN AMP APP.

Okay, you don't need one, but here's the info: an AMP app optimises your site for mobile devices, and this puts your site higher in the search engine rankings—just in case you skimmed the previous chapter on improving store speed!

AMP by Shop Sheriff is a reasonably priced app with a free plan. AMP by Shop Sheriff states it is recommended by the official Google AMP team. It also allows you to hide pages from indexing with the simple use of a tag. This is good SEO practice.

As always, make sure you read the reviews first.

Examples:

Shopify: AMP by Shop Sheriff, The AMP App, Accelerated Mobile Pages, Fire AMP.

WooCommerce: For WordPress: Jetpack, Yoast SEO, AMP WP, PWA for WP and AMP, easy AMP, Schema and Structured Data for WP and AMP, Instantify.

A SALES TAX APP.

(See chapter on Sales Tax.)

Before I mention these apps, Shopify Tax (rolled out early 2023) calculates tax for the US. It will not remit it for you, but it will tell you what and where it is. Therefore, it does the job of some tax apps for the US.

Of course, you might not have a tax liability in the US. Shopify Tax is built-in and is not an app. Word is that Shopify Tax plans to expand to other countries. Shopify has one improvement in beta.

Most sales tax apps charge by the number of orders whether or not those are sales tax <u>exempt</u>. That is, they charge an author with 200 sales of a $4.99 ebook the same as they charge a seller with 200 sales of a $200 item of clothing. There is no way around this. Lovat Compliance, for example, also charges by the number of countries.

TaxJar files internationally for you, but Quaderno while international does not file. Quaderno does handle all your tax calculations and gives you clear, step-by-step instructions on how, where, and when to file. Quaderno sends an automatic notification when you reach a sales tax threshold.

If you are already filing sales tax from another source of income (such as your retailer royalties) and do not want TaxJar to file in your country, you will not have this option. TaxJar will file anyway as it will not allow you to exclude a country. Quaderno does allow you to exclude countries, but, as always, check that this is still the case.

There is also the app EAS EU & UK Compliance which works with Shopify, WooCommerce, and Magento. This app is for the UK and EU VAT only.It automates the EU VAT reports, and you can choose whether to do the filing or let EAS EU & UK Compliance do the filing. The prices range from 0,32€ per transaction (you do the filing) to 1,25€ per transaction (they file). So then, it would not be a good idea to price an audiobook at 99c if you used this app.

Examples of Sales Tax apps:

Shopify: TaxJar; Quaderno, EAS EU & UK Compliance, Lovat Compliance, and others.

Shopify Tax is built in and free until you make a truckload of money. US only. (It will expand.)

WooCommerce: TaxJar, Avalara AvaTax, EAS EU & UK Compliance. There is also Simple Sales Tax (free!) but it only does limited locations.

Check the negative reviews on sales tax apps and see if they all say the same thing.

HEAT MAP / REPLAY APPS.

Do not be tempted to use this as a fix for a hot mess of a store. Get the store right first.

These apps provide live recordings of in-store sessions, that is to say, live visitor tracking. You will be able to see customers looking at products, and you will be able to track the way customers move around your store.

With this information, you can see if there is a sticking point for customers, and fix it.

Examples:

Shopify: RewindCopy, Lucky Orange Heatmaps & Replay, Retter - Heatmaps & Replay.

WooCommerce: Hotjar, Aurora Heatmap, Mouseflow, Matomo.

BACKUP APPS.

These apps generally back up your store on a daily basis. Some apps also help you recover accidentally deleted content.

Examples:

Shopify: Rewind Backups, Goshu: Backup, Restore, Report, or Filey (Filey is free).

WooCommerce: BlogVault, BackWPup, UpdraftPlus.

TOKENGATING APPS.

I discuss tokengating in the next chapter, so I will talk about Tokengating apps there.

. . .

A TIP FOR YOU.

Shopify Chat Support will sometimes (often!) recommend apps when there is a way around it.

Don't go crazy! It's not chocolate!

You don't want to add too many apps as they will slow down your store, and slowing down a store is a very bad thing, a very bad thing indeed. Be judicious when selecting apps.

RESOURCES

QUESTIONS

How will you deliver your digital files?

Which apps/plugins will you add in your store?

RESOURCES

Shopify: apps.shopify.com

WooCommerce: woocommerce.com/products

15. TOKENGATING AND NFTS

““ Token-gating is so much more than
limited edition merch, we're seeing
brands like @doodles use NFTs to build
loyal communities and unlock one-of-a-
kind commerce experiences.

NFTs are changing commerce and
we're ready to power all of it.[1]

— SHOPIFY, MARCH 15, 2022

Don't skim this chapter because it sounds too
futuristic to you. That's what people once said
about televisions and electricity!

> Once a new technology rolls over you,
> if you're not part of the steamroller,
> you're part of the road.
>
> — STEWART BRAND

Imagine you wanted to go on a model railroad journey around a park. You paid the fee at a booth. The attendant handed you a little round token that you had to drop into a machine at the entrance to the train. That token gave you access to the train.

The other day I went to the local recycling centre. I handed the attendant my council voucher, and he handed me a metal token. Upon leaving the recycling centre, cars could go one way and drop a token in a machine to get out for free or could go past another attendant to pay.

This is tokengating—only those with a token are able to go on a train ride, escape from a recycling centre for free, and so on.

Tokengating gives token holders access to exclusive products and content, or special discounts on new products. For the world outside bookselling, tokengating can offer access to store openings or special invitations to events.

Tokengating uses NFTs. An NFT is just another type of token (hence the token in *token*gating), in this case, a non-fungible token. Fungible means something that can be replaced by something identical to it, such as money, gold bars, or cans of food.

Non-fungible means something is unique. A non-fungible token is a unique token.

Many people associate NFTs simply with works of art, but they are a good form of security. Proof of NFT ownership is stored on a blockchain, so token ownership cannot be forged. That means token-gating is secure.

You could make limited editions of your books available only to token holders.

Tokengating apps.

Examples:

Free: Shopthru, AlphaSprouts NFT Power-Ups, Lit Token Access

Paid: NFT Token Gating & Discounts, Taco: NFT Loyalty Automation

NFTs.

Yes, you could even sell NFTs on Shopify! Why not bundle a book with an NFT? And one day soon, you will be able to offer a book as an NFT and receive royalties when that NFT is resold.

Better still, you can even mint your own NFTs with a Shopify app on blockchains such as Ethereum, Solana, Polygon, and Flow, and then sell your NFTs on Shopify.

What does mint mean? When somebody mints an NFT, they are publishing it on the blockchain, making it available for purchase.

I have more good news. You don't need any crypto to sell NFTs on Shopify, and your customers don't need any crypto either. You can accept the usual Shopify methods of payments that you use to sell books. Buyers simply claim their NFTs by email. If the customer doesn't already have a wallet, the process guides them on how to create one.

Shopify has the following NFT minting apps: BCware, Verisart, Dropmint, Fungyy, GigLabs, Vivid Labs, Novel, Nifty Bridge, PERCS Mint, Items, NF Teapot, Venly, and others.

Skip the following if you don't want to go more in-depth:

I should mention that Taco: NFT Loyalty Automation is an NFT airdropping app. An NFT airdrop refers to NFTs that are sent to a web3 wallet for free as a promotion to draw attention to a brand or experience. This app automatically notifies customers who qualify (maybe by dollar value of products bought or number of products bought), and the customers do not pay gas fees (transaction fees). These can be used to offer special products and pricing to customers.

What is a web3 wallet?

A web3 wallet stores your NFTs and digital content in the same way a physical wallet stores your cash and cards. A web3 wallet contains:

1. A public key. This is a link where you can send and receive transactions.

2. A private key. This has to be kept Top Secret! You use it to gain access to funds and to sign new transactions.

3. A Seed Phrase: This is used to generate multiple private keys. It provides access to the other keys and addresses in the wallet.

RESOURCES

QUESTIONS

Have you considered tokengating?

If so, what benefits or products would you offer?

16. 7 WAYS TO SELL FROM YOUR AUTHOR STORE OR WEBSITE

66 Make a customer, not a sale.

— KATHERINE BARCHETTI

I confess there are more than 7 ways, but mentioning a number is good marketing. 7 and 5 are good numbers to mention, 18 not so much. There's plenty of research on this, but let's get back to the 7 ways—ahem, more than 7—ways to sell your book!

It all depends where you are with direct selling right now. I use and recommend Shopify, but I've run through the sales platforms for you here. (Have I mentioned I recommend Shopify?) I do have an affiliate link here, but I would not use anything other than Shopify if you are serious about running a business.

Is it for you?

I have several Shopify stores all of which double up as my websites, but many people integrate their store to their website by adding 'Store' to their menu. Some have a book image with buy buttons to their store as well as to the retailers. You could do this with any storefront and find a theme/template that best matches your site.

If you want to use Shopify as your website, skip to the end of this chapter.

Sure, you can start out with Payhip, but if you want to use BookVault or Lulu Direct to handle print books for you (and don't want to use an API), you will need Shopify or WooCommerce. Book-Vault and Lulu Direct enable you to sell print books from your store without having to ship or keep stock and without an API, they only integrate with Shopify and WooCommerce. Of course, you can always swap to one of those later.

It's super easy to set up preorders with Book-Funnel plus a store you can integrate with BookFunnel.

If you are starting out and don't want to use Shopify and do not want an actual ecommerce business, then Payhip might be a good option for you. So then, you could get your website designer to add 'Store' to your menu, linking to your Payhip store, and you could also have a "Buy Direct from Author" button at the top of your buy links to other retailers. And if you use Books2Read, it now includes a link to Payhip.

If you change your mind down the track, it's possible to migrate from Shopify to WooCommerce (manually or with a migration service or plugin) and vice versa (manually or with a migration service or app).

What can't you sell in a store? Cons?

You cannot sell direct unless you own the rights, and you cannot sell ebooks direct if those ebooks are in KDP Select, that is, exclusive to Amazon.

Sales from your store don't count to hitting lists such as the USA Today Bestseller list.

You won't get bestseller stripes on books in your store.

It's the whole "bank over rank" thing - would you rather have money or glory? (I'd rather have the money!)

There's usually a cost involved, even if it's a small cost.

But first, here's a hot tip!

HOT TIP!

Apply for a PayPal Business account. Once you have it, message PayPal and ask for Micropayments to be enabled.
Micropayments are for digital goods priced up to $10-$12, depending on your country. This makes the PayPal fees very low indeed, generally far lower than any other payment method.
And don't worry, if somebody buys a $20 item, having micropayments enabled will not adversely affect you at all.

Now to the different ways to sell direct. Did I mention I recommend Shopify? You want to use something else? Okay, I tried. Here are some of the storefronts.

1. PAYHIP

Digital - All file formats. "This includes audio files, video files, text files and any file with any extension."

You can offer courses.

Print - no integrations

Integrations - BookFunnel, WordPress, Squarespace, Wix, Weebly, EmailOctopus, ConvertKit.

Price - free plan to $99/month plan (+ payment fees)

Many authors starting to sell direct do so by putting a Buy button on their website and linking to the book's listing on Payhip.

Payhip has a free plan which takes a 5% transaction fee, a Plus Plan which takes a 2% transaction fee, and a Pro Plan which doesn't take any transaction fee at all. Bear in mind that you will still be charged payment processing fees for either PayPal or Stripe.

You can link to one of your products on Payhip from your store, or you can set up a whole store on Payhip.

Payhip offers reviews and bundles. Bundles can be a mix of digital products or even a course and an ebook. Subscriptions are also possible.

Payhip delivers digital content. You can also have BookFunnel deliver the files as well to take advantage of BookFunnel's support.

That's more, Payhip collects and pays all UK and EU VAT.

Payhip is easy.

2. CONVERTKIT (Also an email service provider)
Digital - delivers ebook files
Print - does not offer
Integrations - none
Price - does not charge extra for ecommerce.
Price depends on your number of newsletter subscribers and starts with a free plan (+ payment processing fees)

ConvertKit is known as an email service provider, but it also provides an ecommerce platform for digital goods.

Their payment processor is Stripe. From the ConvertKit website: "Start selling products on our free plan and only be charged a low 3.5%+30c transaction fee. Get paid out every week on Friday."

You can also sell paid newsletter subscriptions on ConvertKit. I mentioned these before, but in case you don't remember, these are high-volume, low-cost subscriptions, currently highly popular. These easily suit non-fiction authors.

3. BOOKFUNNEL
Not a sales platform but oh so good!

BookFunnel is a Delivery Service (ebook and audio) and here's the thing— BookFunnel is a Support Provider.

Integrations - Shopify, WooCommerce, Payhip, Selz, PayPal.

Price - $20 to $250/year if paid annually. Audiobook delivery requires the Midlist plan of $100/year if paid annually. (Send an email to request audio.)

BookFunnel will not deliver a free book on the $20/year plan.

I find BookFunnel invaluable. I have Shopify stores, but I used to use Payhip, and even then, I used BookFunnel for support. How would you explain to a customer that ebooks don't arrive in an envelope at a physical address? That example might sound extreme, but you'll soon find out it isn't all that extreme if you have to handle your own support. Trust me on this!

I only have my sanity thanks to BookFunnel.

You set up a one-time delivery action with the store of your choice on BookFunnel. Then you set up a product page on BookFunnel, upload the files, and then set up a sales action.

If the buyer buys more than one book, Book-Funnel will deliver multiple book links in the one email.

You can deliver preorders with BookFunnel.

4. PAYPAL
Not a sales platform either!
Digital - You can put a PayPal button on your website, integrate with BookFunnel, and hey presto! You have a sales, delivery, and support system!
Print - yes, you have to fulfil.

How does this work? Put a PayPal button on an ebook or audiobook on your website, integrate with BookFunnel, and BookFunnel automatically delivers files.

Setting up PayPal buy buttons on a site is difficult for beginners. However, the BookFunnel part is easy. You can customise the book's download page as well as the email message buyers receive.

As soon as the PayPal payment is processed, buyers are taken to the BookFunnel download link. BookFunnel emails them the link/s as well.

5. LEADPAGES

Digital - integrates with SendOwl (Zapier needed) to deliver digital files

Print - no

Integrations - integrates with Facebook ads, Instagram ads, and Google ads. Several other integrations including mail service providers.

Integrates with Shopify buy buttons (Shopify Starter plan)

Price - Prices start at $37/month which makes it more expensive than Shopify's Basic plan.

Leadpages is for lead magnets and selling digital products and services. It does offer pop-ups and upsell pages as well as thank you pages. Use it with LeadDigits to enable SMS collection.

5. SELZ

Digital - delivers

Print - yes, you fulfil

Integrations - PayPal; BookFunnel

Facebook, Instagram, Google.

Plus several more.

Price - Starts at \$29/month, at which card rates are 2.9% + 30¢. Added transaction fees zero for Selz Pay, but if you want PayPal, it's an extra 2%.

Selz will add and display taxes for you but will not pay them. You have the option to configure business tax rates.

It's not an easy platform.

With Selz, you can integrate to sell on social media platforms.

6. PODIA

Digital - yes
Print - no
Integrations - PayPal
Price - there is a free plan, but it attracts 8% fees and only allows 1 download.
Free to install on your WordPress site, but you have to pay to host your domain.

With Podia, you can sell courses, memberships, consultations, and workshops. It has an email facility and an affiliate program.

Podia doesn't charge payment fees on paid plans, but PayPal or Stripe will charge a standard transaction fee.

7. SELLFY

Digital - yes

Print - no integration

Integrations - print on demand

Price - there is a $0 plan, but it's for up to 10 physical products only. The digital products plan starts at $22/month.

Sellfy has a built-in print on demand, offering t-shirts, hoodies, hats, and mugs. Sellfy delivers digital files such as audio and ebooks. You can sell digital subscriptions through Sellfy.

It automatically translates based on the customer's location. It also optimises for phones.

8. SQUARESPACE

Digital - yes

Print - no integration

Integrations - rudimentary

Price - $16-$52/month

Their cheapest plan does not do ecommerce. Squarespace as a website has a low degree of difficulty. However, the degree of difficulty is high if you want to use it as a store. It will integrate with (non book) print on demand.

9. SQUARE

Digital - yes

Print - no integration

Integrations - Google Product, Instagram, Facebook Shop. Afterpay.

Price - has a free plan, but if you want to remove ads, plans start at $15/month.

Square is set up for ecommerce. It has inbuilt reviews.

10. WIX

Digital - yes

Print - yes, you fulfil

Integrations - Will connect with socials: Facebook, Instagram, Pinterest and more. Print on demand

Price - has a free plan.

You can add a Shopify buy button for around $5 a month to your Wix site.

Wix accepts PayPal, Stripe, Square, and all major credit and debit cards as payment methods.

11. WEEBLY

Digital - yes

Print - no integration

Integrations - some email providers, some tax (not sales tax) apps, Facebook ads.
Price - Free plan to $30/year

Easy to customise and has good analytics, handles coupons and gift cards. Has built-in reviews. Accepts Square, Stripe, or PayPal.

12. THRIVECART (the platform not the app)

Digital - yes
Print - no integration
Integrations - Zapier
Price - It's a one-off fee, usually around $500, depending on current offers.

ThriveCart is a shopping cart platform. It specialises in digital downloads, courses (though videos require a hosting service), and subscription services. It offers upsells and down sells. It offers the facility to name your own price and also offers coupons.

Unlike WooCommerce, it's a hosted service.

The Pro edition has a tiered affiliate program.

13. SAMCART

Digital - Yes, SamCart specialises in digital products
Print - no integration
Integrations - Zapier, many email service providers
Price - $49 - $159/month, with a 20% deduction for paying yearly.

SamCart claims it is easy to set up with no technical knowledge. Like ThriveCart, it's a hosted service.

It specialises in digital downloads, courses, and coaching.

14. EASY DIGITAL DOWNLOADS

Digital - yes
Print - no integration
Integrations - PayPal
Several others including email marketing services.
Price - Prices range from $99/year to $499/year. Free to install on your WordPress site, but you have to pay to host your domain.

Easy Digital Downloads is a WordPress plugin. You can create discount codes and accept payments. It has a shopping cart. It accepts a range of payments including PayPal, Stripe, Apple.

15. GUMROAD

Digital - yes

Print - no integration

Integrations - numerous, including MailerLite, Mailchimp, ActiveCampaign, AWeber, Zendesk, Square, Google Sheets.

Price - Gumroad has no monthly fees. It takes a percentage based on lifetime earnings. It ranges from 9% up to $1,000 ranking to 2.9% for over a million dollars and over. There is also a 30c fee on all transactions.

Gumroad remits VAT and GST. As well as digital downloads, you can sell courses and memberships. It also has an email facility and an affiliate program. With Gumroad, you can offer discount codes.

16. WP FORMS

Digital - yes

Print - no integration

Integrations - PayPal, Stripe, Square, and Authorize.Net.

Several email marketing integrations.

Price - Free to install on your WordPress site, but you have to pay to host your domain. Costs anything from $39/year to $599/year depending on discounts.

WP Forms is a WordPress plugin. It's basic. Far easier to set up than WooCommerce but has nowhere near the capabilities.

17. WOOCOMMERCE
Digital - only with an app
Print - the BookVault integration and the Lulu Direct integration will print and ship
Integrations - PayPal, BookFunnel, Facebook, Instagram, Google, Pinterest.
Plus too many others to mention.
Price - Free to install on your WordPress site, but you have to pay to host your domain. No annual fees.

It's easy if you know how! That is, if you're good with WordPress you'll find it easy, but it will likely be difficult for everybody else.

Transaction fees are different for every country, but it accepts a variety of payment processors.

WooCommerce is an open-source plugin you add to your WordPress site. WordPress is a free and open-source Content Management System (CMS) that was written in PHP code. If this makes sense to you, you'll find it easy. At any rate, it does have a setup wizard. "Help will always be given at Hogwarts, Harry, to those who ask for it." This helpful wizard will show you how to add a payment gateway and select currencies.

WooCommerce offers blogging.

WooCommerce has free themes and plenty of paid themes, whether from WooCommerce or a third party.

While WooCommerce is free to use, you need to pay for a hosting server. With Shopify, this is all done for you.

18. SHOPIFY

Digital - only with an app (but I use BookFunnel)
Print - BookVault integration will print and ship books
Lulu Direct will print and ship books
Integrations - PayPal, BookFunnel, Facebook, Instagram, Google, Pinterest, TikTok, eBay.
Plus too many others to mention.

Price - Shopify Starter Plan is $5 a month, Basic is $29/month, Shopify is $79/month, Advanced is $299/month, with deductions for paying annually. There are higher level plans as well.

Shopify is the second biggest storefront in the world, second only to Amazon.

Shopify Starter includes unlimited product pages, shopping cart, checkout, customer contact page, use of discount codes, Shopify Inbox, Shopify order management as well as Linkpop. (There was a Shopify Lite plan, but Starter replaced it mid 2022.) It does not include POS.

Shopify provides hosting and a Secure Sockets Layer (SSL) certificate. It's usually easy to transfer your existing domain name to Shopify, but you can buy one from them.

Shopify is easy and takes no time at all to set up. You can start by choosing a free theme. In fact, I suggest starting by using a free theme, even if you intend to buy a paid theme later on. It's best to learn the ropes on a free theme, as when you buy a theme later, it will make sense to you. Bear in mind that many of the 7 and 8 figure brands use the free default theme.

Until you're making one million dollars a year (and maybe even after that) on the one store, the Basic plan is all you need.

Shopify Tax is built-in and tells you if you have a tax liability in the US. It also tells you how much it is.

If you opt to use Shopify Payments, you can accept online payments immediately. It's easy to add PayPal as well, and even crypto.

Shopify also supports point-of-sale transactions, which is a great help if you sell at conventions or shows like Supernova or Comicon (or whatever it is called in your part of the world).

Shopify has, as standard, an abandoned cart recovery feature and will send email reminders.

Shopify offers blogging.

Until late 2022, to set your own prices for different countries you needed to be on the Shopify Advanced plan ($299/month). I'm not talking about currency conversion. When I sell a $4.99 ebook on the retailers in the USA, I set the price to $4.99 in Australia and $4.99 in New Zealand. The currency conversion would price this at over $7 in Australia and around $8 in New Zealand.

Now you can do this for free with Shopify Markets, usually available automatically to people in most countries. Prior to that, only way you could set your own international prices on Shopify was to pay for the Advanced plan or get a multi-currency app, and I found those had limitations.

Using Shopify as your website.

It's quite easy to do this!

You can add links to your book on all the retailers on each book's product page.

Most themes come with a Contact form, a Privacy Policy page, and a Terms & Conditions page. If your theme is lacking anything, it's easy to add whatever you like to Pages, and it's super easy to add a page to the header and footer menus.

You can have a reading order page with a link to a printable pdf.

You can move the sales button from any product page you wish.

You can have a Shopify store that looks just like a website.

RESOURCES

QUESTIONS

Have you applied for PayPal Micropayments?

Have you decided which storefront to use?

RESOURCES

YouTube

From Selling E-Books To $400M+ Industry Leading Business, with Tobi Pearce (Sweat)

youtube.com/watch?v=NXzKuhbMNno

17. LET'S GET LEGAL!

> The minute you get away from fundamentals – whether it's proper technique, work ethic or mental preparation – the bottom can fall out of your game, your schoolwork, your job, whatever you're doing.
>
> — MICHAEL JORDAN

Amazon reviews.

It's not legal to import Amazon reviews to your store without the express permission of the reviewer. The reviewer owns the copyright of reviews on storefronts such as Amazon. This applies everywhere, not just to Amazon.

You cannot legally import reviews to your store (whether via a review app or any other means) without that reviewer's specific permission. You cannot even use a review (without permission) in your product description as you do not own the copyright.[1]

❝ Can I use a good review for my product description?

No. The reviewer owns the copyright of the review.

Yes, I know some review apps offer this service, but that doesn't change the facts. Just because you can do it doesn't mean it's legal. Otherwise, bank robbers would not be in prison.

KDP Select/Kindle Unlimited.

If your ebooks are in Select, you cannot put them wide or sell them in your store.

However, you can sell print books and/or audio (even if the ebook version is in Select).

Sales tax.

You can't ignore it and hope it will go away. See the chapter on sales tax.

Credit Card fraud.

Shopify's fraud analysis helps you identify orders that could be fraudulent in order to avoid potential chargebacks. You are able to review high-risk orders.

If you have Shopify Payments (recommended! And it's free!), then fraud analysis includes the following: indicators, support for third-party fraud apps (such as Fraud Filter, ClearSale Fraud Protection) fraud recommendations.

On WooCommerce, you can install the Fraud Prevention Module.

I speak more about this in the chapter, Accepting Payments.

SMS marketing.

You must have the subscriber's explicit permission to market to them. Having a pre-checked box is not explicit permission.

Email marketing, General Data Protection Regulation (GPDR).

You also need to collect specific consent when marketing to anybody in Europe. Consent must be freely given and not as an exchange for goods or services (paid or free). Again, having a pre-checked box is not explicit permission. An unsubscribe option should always be provided. You can read more on the official GPDR site.

RESOURCES

QUESTIONS

Have you checked to see if your store is compliant?

If your store doesn't offer fraud prevention, what measures can you take?

RESOURCES

Website

12 Testimonial Guidelines to Ensure You're Not Breaking the Law

https://boast.io/testimonial-guidelines-ensure-youre-not-breaking-law/

18. CASE STUDIES

I asked the following authors for feedback about their selling direct experiences.

Samantha Price
samanthapriceauthor.com
Shopify

1. What prompted you to sell direct?

I'll tell you a quick story. Two days after I had a BookBub Featured Deal on a certain book, Amazon suppressed it and asked me to show them proof that I had the proper authority to use the images on the cover.

I sent them what they asked for, and about a week later, my book was back up for sale. I asked them if they'd reimburse me for the lost income, but I got no reply. No surprise there.

Don't get me wrong. I love Amazon. They've been good to me.

But what if they had suppressed all my books or shut down my whole account? That's scary for an author who's solely in KU.

This didn't prompt me to sell direct, but it certainly reinforced that I was doing the right thing.

I was excited about selling direct as soon as I learned about the Lulu Direct integration with Shopify. The fact that Lulu Direct handles all the packaging and postage of the paperbacks was a game changer for me.

I've had many readers wanting to buy paperbacks directly from me, but it wasn't practical to hold stock and make trips to the Post Office. I'd rather spend the time writing. Now, I've got Lulu Direct doing it all for me.

2. What platform do you use?

Shopify, and I now use the store as my website.

3. What hurdles have you faced?

It's taking a long time to load my books onto the platform. Including paperbacks, large prints, audiobooks, box set audiobooks, and omnibuses, I would have probably over 600 products. With my writing schedule, I've only been able to add one or two a day.

Getting to know my way around Shopify was also a learning curve.

4. What have you found useful?

The customer info is wonderful. When selling direct, you know who your customer is. With Amazon, readers can 'follow' me, but Amazon won't even give me some basic information, such as how many followers I have.

At the very least, I want basic information about my readers.

One thing I also love is Klaviyo (email and SMS marketing). I'm amazed at what it can do and the way it segments everything for you. I'm not using it to the fullest yet, but it's on the to-do list.

5. What are your objectives in selling direct?

For the readers to have a more direct experience by buying straight from me, the author.

I'm also hoping to reach a new segment of readers.

6. Anything else you would like to add about the experience?

I'm excited about the potential and scope there is with Shopify.

C.A. Phipps
C.A. Phipps
Shopify

1. What prompted you to sell direct?

Mainly to move away from KU, and also I see it as a positive way to move my career forward with more control over my business.

2. What platform do you use?

Shopify

3. What hurdles have you faced?

Time has been the main hurdle as it is a steep learning curve, followed by where and how to advertise.

4. What have you found useful?

Morgana's guide. Without that I would have floundered!

5. What are your objectives in selling direct?

To make more money and have ease of pricing control.

6. Anything else you would like to add about the experience?

Tackling a little every day I managed to get all my paperbacks and audio loaded for my 12 cozy mysteries while I wait for my ebooks to come out of KU.

That done, I made the decision to include my romance pen name which has 18 books wide already. I think this will be cost-effective by giving me twice the products.

Kate Hunt

Kate Hunt Romance
Shopify

1. What prompted you to sell direct?

Selling direct has been on my mind for a while now, but hearing success stories from other authors definitely prompted me to take the leap myself. It's a step toward not being so reliant on other retailers, and it also allows me to have far greater control over how my books are sold and the types of sales and promotions I offer my readers. A higher profit margin is also a huge plus, since it means I can invest more money back into my business.

2. What platform do you use?

I'm using Shopify, integrated with BookFunnel to deliver my ebooks. I'm very happy with that setup and would recommend it to anyone.

3. What hurdles have you faced?

My biggest challenge so far has been getting readers to buy on a platform besides Amazon. I'm hoping there will be less resistance to buying direct as more and more authors offer it as an option and readers become used to it.

4. What have you found useful?

Before launching, I put a lot of thought into making my website as easy to use as possible. Then, when I announced my shop's launch, I offered one of my books for free as a way to encourage readers to try out my shop. I'm also planning on offering special discounts and exclusive content on my website in the future. Something I learned when researching selling direct was that simply offering your books for purchase isn't necessarily enough; many readers need an incentive to buy from you.

5. What are your objectives in selling direct?

One of my objectives is to develop a more direct relationship with my readers. In terms of monetary goals, my first big goal is to make $1,000 per month through my website. My shoot-for-the-moon goal is to someday be earning more through my website than what I earn from Amazon.

6. Anything else you would like to add about the experience?

I didn't expect it to feel so empowering to launch my own website! Even before my first sale came in, I got such a rush from seeing my own little bookshop exist in the world. I think every author should get to experience that same feeling.

Victoria LK Williams
Victoria LK Williams
Payhip

1. What prompted you to sell direct?

The main reason I decided to sell direct was control. I want to adjust my pricing and run specials for my readers without jumping through hoops of the big 5. I also did not want to have all my sales "in one basket" at the same time that I was giving them 35% of my sales revenue.

2. What platform do you use?

I am currently using Payhip. It was easy to set up and links with BookFunnel. It may not have all the bells and whistles as Shopify, but it allows me to offer discounts and sales incentives to my readers.

3. What hurdles have you faced?

The main hurdle for me has been the time to create the store and getting my readers to go there instead of Amazon. Habits are hard to break for readers, and myself. I often forget to push my own site.

4. What have you found useful?

The coupons for discounts I can create for my readers. This is something I will offer in my news-letter only, and for a limited time.

5. What hurdles have you found in selling direct?

It is so new. The readers hesitate to veer away from the sites they know like Amazon. I have yet to figure out how to push my books from Payhip. One nice thing is if you are using D2D, they have a Payhip link and you can move that to be the 1st link to click on-moving it ahead of the big 5 retailers.

6. Anything else you would like to add about the experience?

This is a new form of sales for indies and like everything else, we are going to have to build on each sale. I do know that every newsletter with a coupon makes a few direct sales, and that's a good start.

Misty Evans Books/ Nyx Halliwell Books
Misty Evans Books
Nyx Halliwell Books
WooCommerce

1. What prompted you to sell direct?

I have always been a DIY type of person, especially when it comes to my business. Selling direct is right up my alley because I can control the way my books are distributed and give less of my profits to a middleman.

This is my livelihood, so I'm always exploring new revenue streams, and this is a strategic option that works for me.

2. What platform do you use?

My two websites (I have two pen names) are WordPress and I use WooCommerce with PayPal.

3. What hurdles have you faced?

I am not a techie person, so I hired my son, who is, to help me. He designed one of my websites and walked me through connecting WooCommerce to both. He's set up multiple authors with direct buy stores and is familiar with the various platforms. If I encounter something I can't figure out via trial and error or a YouTube video, I can depend on him to show me how to do it.

A second challenge was encouraging readers to use the direct buy option. This is a work in progress, but I'm seeing income increase each month as people become more comfortable using it.

4. What have you found useful?

BookFunnel has been one of the keys to success for me. They have a user friendly dashboard, great customer service, and have added additional delivery options, such as audiobooks.

Also, offering fans early releases and discounts has driven more buyers to my sites.

5. What are your objectives in selling direct?

Supporting my family and making readers happy. Win-win! I'm able to offer fans special collections I don't put on retailers, lower prices on many of my books, and early releases. My VIP readers love to get their hands on stories early, and I'm able to pass on savings since I don't have to cough up 30% or more to retailers.

6. Anything else you would like to add about the experience?

I see direct sales as empowering for authors, and I believe it will continue to grow.

I remember when the traditional publishing world claimed ebooks were a fad, then that indie publishing was a joke. I believed differently, knowing that removing the gatekeepers from the equation was good for all of us.

Selling direct gives us another connection to our readers that benefits everyone.

P.A. Mason
P.A. Mason
Shopify

1. What prompted you to sell direct?

I love being an indie author—to the point that I've never submitted a query letter to an agent or publisher. For me, selling direct feels like the pinnacle of being indie. Now I'm not only the author, publisher, and the marketing team but also the book retailer. And like most things, this extra work gives me more control and the benefit of data to inform my business decisions.

2. What platform do you use?

I was lucky enough to stumble across a digital adaption grant in my home state in Australia which partnered with Shopify. At that point I already had a Payhip store, but I made the switch and am very glad I did. I purchased a three year basic subscription with the grant which gave me some extra perks including live shipping rates from third party apps like Lulu and Printify.

3. What hurdles have you faced?

Selling direct is definitely a learning curve, and it takes time to figure out the platform. I think it's important to see that time as an investment, but also to balance it against the WIBBOW principle. As with most new shiny things, it's easy to get caught up doing the 80% busy work. Living in Australia is also a hurdle even in an international market when it can take over a month to have a sample arrive in the post if you set things up to cater for a US market.

4. What have you found useful?

Definitely finding Morgana's Authors Selling Direct Facebook group. When you first look at your store dashboard, you have about a million questions running through your mind. I think I read almost every post when I joined and picked up so many tips which I imagine are all included in these pages. But it's more than that. It's a very supportive environment, and it's nice to feel like you're part of a team when you venture out into the Wild West of indie publishing.

5. What are your objectives in selling direct?

I want to convince as many of my existing readers to buy direct as I can. We know as authors that we shouldn't build our entire platform on turf we don't own—places like social media—which is why we all run newsletters. For me, the same goes with selling books. I'm at the start of my career, so I have the *opportunity* to start building this now and not worry about cannibalizing sales on Amazon. This mindset shift is important. I would never have considered myself 'ready' for selling direct until I was making a good living with a big reader-ship. Now, I realize this store is something that can grow alongside me.

6. Anything else you would like to add about the experience?

Only that I think Shopify makes so many things possible in one place. We are always looking for tools to help us save time, and I never imagined we were already close enough tech-wise to sell not only eBooks direct but also audiobooks—with a nod to BookFunnel of course—and print with the support of Lulu POD. But the store is only limited by your imagination. I put out a free novella a while ago with a third party tipping service for people who wanted to throw some money in. Now, I can do that seamlessly with tipping in the store. That's just one of many ideas I'm looking forward to testing out.

19. INTERNATIONAL CURRENCIES

66 A big business starts small.

— RICHARD BRANSON

Setting up countries and pricing will depend on whether you're using Payhip, Shopify, WooCommerce or so on.

If you solely want a currency conversion to show in separate countries' currencies and set your own prices, Shopify does that for free with Shopify Markets. You can also do that with a WooCommerce plugin. WooCommerce has a plugin for pricing by country that is $49 annually.

Shopify Markets allows you to sell in 133 different countries. It will convert the currency of your default currency and allow you to sell in the target country's own currency. Better still, you can set your own prices for each product in each country if you wish.

Why would you need to set different prices for countries? Well, I'm an Aussie. If I sell a $4.99 USD ebook on a US retailer, I also price that book at $4.99 Aussie money in Australia and $4.99 New Zealand money in New Zealand. A currency conversion would make that $4.99 USD book around $7.50 in Australia and around $8 in New Zealand.

Yes, such things do matter to those of us Down Under. In Brisbane, a latte costs around $5. I wouldn't pay $7.50 for a latte just because that's what it would be worth in US currency conversion. Make sense? Maybe I needed another $5 coffee before explaining.

Rounding off prices.

In Shopify, go to Settings > Markets > Preferences. Select Price Rounding and save.

TIP.

Do not confuse currency conversion with setting your own prices. Shopify Markets does automatic currency conversion and also allows you to set your prices. It's free and comes as the default.

RESOURCES

QUESTIONS

What is your main market? US, UK, AU, CA, or NZ?

Are there any countries you wish to exclude?

How will you handle international currencies?

RESOURCES (I have not tried the below plugins. They are here for your information only.)

WooCommerce.

Currency Switcher https://woocommerce.com/products/currency-switcher-for-woocommerce/

Multi-currency https://woocommerce.com/products/multi-currency

20. WHAT YOU NEED TO START A STORE

66 Dream big. Start Small.

But most of all, start.

— SIMON SINEK

It's easier to move to selling direct if you have a large newsletter list or even a smaller but nicely engaged newsletter list. Still, there are benefits to having even one book with a direct buy button on your website. As Confucius said, "The journey of 1000 miles begins with the first step."

It's best to start and learn on the way. Don't wait for perfection.

· · ·

WHAT DO YOU NEED TO SELL DIRECT?

A storefront or a buy button.

A sales system - to take the money

A delivery system - to deliver the books:

1. digital

2. print books

Get sales tax sorted.

Set up countries and pricing.

Optional - set up Support (such as BookFunnel, although I'd call this necessary, not optional)

A BREAKDOWN OF THE NECESSITIES.

Open a PayPal Business account. Apply for PayPal micropayments.

Choose a storefront or a product landing page.

Start your free trial if on Shopify. For other storefronts, open an account.

Add products.

Set up delivery - and support if you wish.

Customise your store's appearance.

Set up your domain.

Choose payment providers.

Set up email and/or SMS marketing.

Set up sales tax.

Launch your store.

OPTIONAL THINGS TO DO.

Set up BookFunnel for Support for digital downloads (ebooks and audiobooks)

RESOURCES

QUESTIONS

New to Direct Selling:

Do you have:

A storefront or a buy button

A sales system - to take the money

A delivery system - to deliver the books:

1. digital

2. print books?

Already Selling Direct:

Have you added apps/plugins?

Have you set up email and/or SMS marketing?

RESOURCES

Books

Good to Great: Why Some Companies Make the Leap and Others Don't, Jim Collins.

P.S. You're a Genius: An Unconventional Guide To Finding Your Innate Gifts (Even When You Feel Like You Have None), Kelly Trach

Undaunted: Overcoming Doubts and Doubters, Kara Goldin

21. NO MONEY TO START A STORE? DO THIS!

> Every day is a bank account, and time is our currency. No one is rich, no one is poor, we've got 24 hours each.

— CHRISTOPHER RICE

You don't have enough money to start a store? All is good! There are things you can do.

First, not having enough money falls into two camps.

1. You actually don't have any money. (Been there, done that!)

2. You do have money, but you do not want to allocate money to a store until you make enough to cover your costs.

I will address both of these separately as they are completely different issues.

1. You actually don't have any money.

Okay, so you have at least one book on the retailers. You're scratching to pay the bills. What can you do?

For a start, if the ebooks are in Kindle Select, put them wide. Fast. Seriously. People who read wide are happier to buy from an online bookstore than people in Kindle Unlimited. There is far better readthrough from a first in series free for wide (non-Amazon retailers such as Nook, Kobo, GooglePlay, Apple) than on Select.

Remember, other retailers are a funnel to your store! Find a way to let Apple know about your book. If you are via an aggregator (such as Draft2Digital), email their Support to ask how to get an Apple promo. (It's free.) If you are direct to Apple, email their Support constantly asking for the email of a rep. They might keep telling you they don't have reps, but persist until they give you a rep's email. Once you have that rep's email, request that they send you the promotion form.

What do you need to start a store? If you are tech savvy and have or can start a WordPress site, you're in luck. That's free. Then you can use the WooCommerce plugin for free to set up a store. The expense here is web hosting.

You could use Payhip. They have a free plan. You can set up a nice storefront with Payhip and they will deliver digital files for you. (No upfront cost; they take a transaction fee.)

If you already have a website, you can link to Payhip.

If you don't have a newsletter list yet, start one ASAP. Like, yesterday. Most of the big email service providers have a free plan generally for up to 1000 subscribers. Whatever you do, don't go with a lesser-known mail service provider for the sole reason its advanced plans look cheap. That is false economy on steroids. Also, make use of any free trial to see if it suits.

For ebooks, if you can stretch to BookFunnel's $20 a year plan for Support and delivery on ebook files, that's good. If not, you can handle your own support when starting off. I suggest explaining as much as you can on the product page. Some people won't read it, but most will, and that will save you work. And when you get to a place where you are handling too many support requests, you will be making enough money to go on a Book-Funnel plan.

Now, let's look at your back matter. If you write in a series, link to the next book in the series at the end of each book. You can link to the retailers, such as by linking to Books2Read, and under that, have the words, "Or buy at a discount here" and link to the book in your store.

I almost forgot. Payhip accepts PayPal and Stripe. I'll mention PayPal micropayments again. You will save money if you apply for micropayments. It's completely free! You must apply for a PayPal Business account first. (Also free.) Once you have it, message PayPal and request they enable PayPal micropayments. These apply to digital goods $10 to $12 (or so, depending on your country) and under. It's by far the cheapest transaction fee of all. Normal PayPal rates will apply to anything over that as well as to physical goods.

This is by far the best option in my view! If you're not completely broke and can afford $5/month, Shopify Starter is another option. You do not get an actual store with Shopify Starter, but you do get unlimited product pages, checkout, other features, and can use Shopify buy buttons on your website and on social media.

You can integrate with BookVault or Lulu Direct which will print and ship your print books. You will either have to pay Shopify a fee to enable Third-party shipping rates or pay for any Shopify plan a year in advance. After the customer pays you for the book, Lulu Direct deducts their costs. With BookVault, you put money into your account (from £12 - around $12 USD - to whatever you wish) to cover upcoming costs. BookVault and Lulu Direct ship all over the world from local printers.

With Shopify Starter, you can use the Facebook, Instagram, TikTok, Google, and Pinterest apps for free, and your sales products can appear on these platforms for free. With Shopify, you can send your products to social feeds for free.

At any rate, if you are watching the dollars, you can make the most of social media.

If you are friends with other authors, ask for a newsletter swap. It's better to swap with wide authors, but if you can only find KDP Select authors, that's better than nothing, and it's free. Link to a book in your store. Make it a good discount.

Joint promotions are free. Find one of those. Again, it's better if you do it with wide authors.

Back to the newsletters. Develop a relationship with your customers. Give them a glimpse into your life. Show them a photo of a plant you are trying to grow. If you are a runner and have sprained your ankle, show them photos of your injured foot. Pet photos work well too. You can also ask a question as it helps your mail rating to have conversations. The more personable you are, the more people will respond to you. There's a reason reality TV is so popular. You need to get people on your list, but you need to keep them happy and keep them there!

2. You have some money, but you do not want to allocate money to a store until you make enough to cover your costs.

I always hear authors say that they don't want to pay for a store or a store upgrade until they start making money from selling books direct. That is a kind of paradox. It's like showing somebody a piece of paper, on one side of which you have written, "The statement on the other side of this paper is true," and on the other side, you have written, "The statement on the other side of this paper is false."

It's a time paradox, like when Professor Marius was inspired to construct K9 Mark I after seeing K9 Mark III, which was built by Doctor Who after he saw K9 Mark I.

The money needs to come in to pay for the store; the store products need to sell; you need visibility (usually prompted by your marketing efforts) for your store to sell products. Sounds like a temporal loop!

Many authors want to have a successful store without putting time or money into it.

Of course, you can carry out the free efforts mentioned above, but if you are not financially skint, it would be so much faster and more efficient to run your store like a business.

Imagine somebody in the non-author world who is setting up a new brick and mortar business. Let's say shoes. Does the seller sit on a bench in the park under a tree and show a pair of shoes to passers-by? Does the shoe seller say they will not put any money into their business until they have sold enough shoes to cover costs?

No, the seller sets up a store in the best location the seller can afford. Selling on a busy street is preferable to selling down a back alley with no passing trade. The seller invests in the business. However, authors often do the opposite. They want the business to be making money before they will invest in it.

As authors selling direct, we are business people running a business. Sure, it's fine to start off small, but it's good to invest in your business. Have a business plan. Don't simply be hopeful—do something about it.

RESOURCES

QUESTIONS

No Money:

Have you chosen a storefront?

Do you have a mail service provider?

Have you changed your back matter to include your store?

Have you contacted other authors about joint promotions?

Have money but don't like to spend it:

How can you change your mindset to start to treat selling direct as a business?

RESOURCES

Books

Year of Yes, Shonda Rhimes

CEO of My Soul, Nicole Cober

The Lean Startup, Eric Ries

Think and Grow Rich, Napoleon Hill

22. A HOT MESS?

> When I write an advertisement, I don't want you to tell me that you find it 'creative.' I want you to find it so interesting that you buy the product.

— DAVID OGILVY, OGILVY ON
ADVERTISING

Back when I worked in the ad agency as a copywriter and layout artist (I didn't draw any artwork by the way; I laid out the precise format of the ad), we used to call horribly messy, badly laid out ads "Supermarket ads." (Not to be confused with Circus Layout for those in the know!)

This was before the internet. Certain supermarkets took out full-page newspaper ads to sell groceries. These pages were a hot mess. Everything was crammed in. The supermarkets wanted to get every last bit of information about way too many items onto that page. There was no sense of order.

Your store needs to have a sense of order. It needs to look clean. Otherwise, it will look unprofessional.

Don't have several different fonts. A good rule of thumb is to stick to two.

Without getting into the Golden Ratio, the Golden Spiral, and the Grid layout, you should simply take care not to cram all your books together. White space is important too.

You don't need a fancy store and you certainly shouldn't over design. Check out the stores of some major ecommerce businesses.

If you use a review app, make sure you like the aesthetic. Messy review apps do the store no favours. (And remember, it is illegal to use a review without the reviewer's permission.)

Decide on your branding, and make sure your store aligns with your branding. Review apps and marketing apps will integrate with your brand.

There should be a minimal number of clicks to get to your products. However, this has to be weighed against setting out your products in a clear and simple order. The more products you have, the more of a challenge this will prove.

Draw your store's site plan on a piece of paper. Yes, old school! Make a list of categories and subcategories. Decide where to put all your content.

You simply must have information which will hook the customer above the fold.

This is to hook them on your book with your blurb. It is not to tell them how to download the book. The download information needs to be below the fold.

And to add to that, if you over-tell somebody something, it causes suspicion. This is basic buyer psychology. I recommend placing the download information in collapsible rows near the bottom of the page.

The hook should be above the fold. Nobody gives a second thought as to how to download something if they don't want to buy it in the first place. That's why people need to be interested in the product first, and it is essential that the hook and not the download information.is above the fold

Time and time again, I see download information above the fold. This is a serious and basic error.

Also, there is no need for an image showing how to download digital content. Put it in collapsible boxes where people can find it if they wish.

Google indexes those images, and they will appear in searches for your book, and also on Google images and on Pinterest searches instead of your book cover. Thus, a download image is a problem for SEO.

There is plenty of evidence to suggest that telling somebody how to download something in an unnecessary and over-the-top manner places suspicion in their mind. Again, buyer psychology 101.

It is advisable to have the word 'ebook' in ebook product titles, as well as an ebook image, not a paperback or 3D cover, on ebook product pages. I have even seen paperback 3D images on ebook product pages - avoid this at all costs!

Instead of trying to do unusual things, get the basics right first. Remove the quantity selector from digital product pages, remove the 'shipping will be calculated at checkout' from digital product pages, and avoid the least converting buy button colour. And if you feel the urge to do something which is unusual for ecommerce, test it, but the site has to have been running for a while, and all the basics must be correct and in place first.

A customer typically takes 7 seconds to make a buying decision. If this person is looking at numerous images of your fiction book, or worse still at images showing how to download it, there is less time to read the hook. If you want to add extra images to your fiction book product page – and there is zero evidence to suggest that this helps (and remember the 7 seconds - the important info is the hook in text), but you can test it – again, only after the store has been running for a while and all the basics are correct – but certainly do not have one of those images of how to download.

The following image was supplied to me by an author who as horrified to see her download images flooding google searches for her book. She removed the images at once, but the images still appeared 6 months later, as in the following images. Author wishes to remain anonymous so I have hidden all reference to her books.

The image on the left appeared in a google search for the author's name, and the image on the right appeared when the author searched her name on Pinterest.

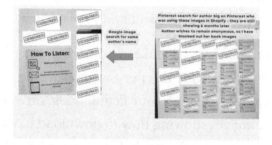

RESOURCES

QUESTIONS

Have you drawn a site plan of your store?

Have you made a list of categories and subcategories. Have you decided where to put all your
content? Will you group ebooks separately? Will
you group series separately? Will you have collection of ebooks in one series, a collection of paperbacks in the same series, and so on?

RESOURCES

Books

Positioning, the Battle For Your Mind, Ries and Trout.

Ogilvy on Advertisement, David Ogilvy.

This Is Marketing: You Can't Be Seen Until You Learn to See, Seth Godin.

SOME SHOPIFY STORES FOR YOU TO STUDY

66 I founded The Oodie in 2018 and since then, I've started over 7 Shopify brands worth over $250 million under my own company - Davie Group.

— DAVIE FOGARTY

Here is a cross sample of some highly successful Shopify stores.

Check them out. Check out whether they use pop-ups, sign up forms, and look at the general aesthetic. Do they use offers?

If they have pop-ups, see whether they pop up immediately or after a delay. If a delay, how many seconds?

What do you think of their review apps?

Do they use bundles?

How do they handle social proof?

What policies are shown in their footers?

Bulletproof. https://www.bulletproof.com/

Jeffree Star Cosmetics. https://jeffreestarcosmetics.com/

Taylor Stitch. https://www.taylorstitch.com/

Cupshe. https://www.cupshe.com/

The Oodie. https://theoodie.com/

ColourPop. https://colourpop.com/

G FUEL Energy Formula. https://gfuel.com/

Fashion Nova. https://www.fashionnova.com/

Sephora. https://www.sephora.com/

Poosh. https://poosh.com/

Skkn by Kim. https://skknbykim.com/

Rebecca Minkoff. https://www.rebeccaminkoff.com/

Kylie Cosmetics. https://kyliecosmetics.com/

Victoria Beckham Beauty. https://www.victori-abeckhambeauty.com/

Ruggable. https://ruggable.com/

L'ange Hair. https://langehair.com/

Raycon. https://rayconglobal.com/

BioLite Energy. https://www.bioliteenergy.com/

Tesla. https://www.tesla.com/

Gymshark. https://www.gymshark.com/

Allbirds. https://www.allbirds.com/

MVMT watches. https://www.mvmt.com/

Bootea. https://www.bootea.com/

Beardbrand. https://www.beardbrand.com/

Luxy Hair. https://www.luxyhair.com/

The Ridge Wallet. https://ridgewallet.com.au/

Nerdwax. https://nerdwax.com/

WP Standard. https://wpstandard.com/

Fangamer. https://www.fangamer.com/

Spigen. https://www.spigen.com/

Miracle by Aloft. https://www.miraclebrand.co/

Tattly. https://tattly.com/

Natural Baby Shower. https://www.natural-babyshower.co.uk/

23. MERCHANDISE

> 66 Merchandising, merchandising, where
> the real money from the movie is made.

— MASTER YOGURT, SPACEBALLS

What is the difference between dropshipping and print on demand?

With print on demand, you can customise the products, whereas with dropshipping, you cannot. For example, with (non-book) print on demand you can sell coffee mugs to which you have added your own design (an easy online process, I might add).

You need to be careful here, as you need a commercial licence for designs on print on demand products. This is not the same licence you need for images on covers.

Merchandise goes nicely with books.

Write dog cozy mysteries? You could bundle a dog bowl or dog bed with a book. Or maybe a pair of socks imprinted with your character. I have a cozy mystery series featuring a wombat by the name of Persnickle, and I used to bundle a book with Persnickle-covered socks. (I paid an artist to design my characters' images.)

Whatever your genre, there will be merch that suits. Just think—what merch goes well with your genre?

Choosing a print on demand app/plugin.

Some things to consider:

What is their returns and refunds policy?

Do they ship from several locations or only from one? If they only ship from the US and you have customers in the UK, this could be a problem.

Some print and ship from 3 locations, whichever is closer to the customer. This will vary between products. For example, a print on demand company will typically have several products that print from one location and other products that ship from multiple locations. Be aware that print quality is likely to vary between the printer locations.

What is the cost? Many are free, but some do charge a yearly fee.

What is their customer service like? Read plenty of reviews.

What are the prices of their products? Some are significantly expensive.

Examples of print on demand apps/plugins.

Printify, Printful, Gooten, Eprolo, Gelato, Contrado, Printy6, Twofifteen, Sprocket, SPOD, Jetprint, Artshiney.

RESOURCES

QUESTIONS

Will you offer merchandise?

If so, which print-on-demand app/plugin will you use?

What products will you sell?

TO DO

Make a list of print on demand companies. Does one company offer every product you wish to sell? If so, are the prices reasonable? Does it ship from the country of your main market?

RESOURCES

Book

Start With Why, Simon Sinek.

24. SELLING PRINT BOOKS

> How you sell has become more important than what you sell.

— MATTHEW DIXON & BRENT ADAMSON, CHALLENGER SALE

There are 4 options for selling print books from your site:

1. You fulfil. This means you have the books printed, and you are responsible for the shipping as well as any warehousing if necessary.

2. You fulfil, but you use Amazon or IngramSpark (or an alternative) for shipping. When somebody buys from your store you ship the book to their

address from Amazon (an author copy) or from IngramSpark.

3. You use a third party such as BookVault or Lulu Direct to print and fulfil. This means you hold no stock; you do no shipping. No running to the post office. It's all hands off. All you do is upload your books online.

4. You use a combination of the above.

It's absolutely your choice. There is no wrong or right way.

You save money if you yourself fulfil print (options 1 or 2) as you have higher profit margins, but you save time using a third party. Another deciding factor is your location. I'm Aussie, and the cost of shipping books out of Australia is astronomical. However, Aussies and other non-US, non-UK authors might find Option 2 attractive.

If you are in a location that dictates that it's not cost-effective to ship signed books, a possible work-around would be to bundle a book shipped by BookVault or Lulu Direct with a bookplate you have signed. You would have to ship the signed bookplates, but the shipping costs would be minimal.

Your situation could well be different. Some authors use warehouses for their print books and therefore do the fulfilling.

There is also the combination method where you could use a third party for most of your books, but you fulfil signed books or special edition books such as hardcovers with sprayed edges.

YOU HAVE THE BOOKS PRINTED AND YOU DO THE SHIPPING.

If you sell large numbers of print books, it's often cheaper to do an offset print run, but offset runs generally start at 1,000 copies. Printing in China is usually the cheapest. If you do that, depending on your country, you might have to pay a Customs Clearance Agent to clear the books into the country. There will also likely be customs duties to pay. These will have to be factored into your costs, as will time if you go the cheaper way of transporting your books from an international printer by ship rather than by air.

Offset printers generally have a wider variety of paper choices and can generally offer covers with foil, embossing, or spot UV. Some even offer sprayed edges.

Digital runs can be done in any numbers.

If you decide on a smaller digital run, you could have books printed by any of the companies mentioned below or even pay for Amazon author copies.

If you want to sell print books and have them shipped internationally at reasonable local shipping rates without your physical involvement, the two main options are BookVault and Lulu Direct.

BOOKVAULT.

BookVault integrates with Shopify, WooCommerce, and Wix, and has an API.

BookVault offers preorders for print and does all standard sizes as well as offering custom sizing. BookVault offers perfect bound (paperback), case bound PPC (hardcover), case bound cloth (hardcover), saddle stitch, spiral bound, and Wire-O bound. They also offer hardcovers with cloth covers and foil blocking. Ribbons and more foil options will be available from early 2024.

BookVault's printing costs are around the same as KDP author copies, both of which are around the cost of Lulu Direct's printing costs. However,

BookVault does have a set up fee per title or a monthly plan. To avoid paying that, an author can pay the monthly plan, upload all their books, and then downgrade to the free plan. Also, if you are a member of ALLi (Alliance of Independent Authors), you have access to a limited number of free codes per month. Also, students of my course, Authors Selling Direct on Shopify, have free uploads.

You can also select to have BookVault distribute to certain retailers such as Gardners. You can even get your Spiral Bound book on Amazon through BookVault.

If you don't want to upload to BookVault, Book-Vault will import all your books for a set fee per title.

BookVault's quality is exceptional.

You don't need your own ISBN to sell through BookVault.

LULU DIRECT.

Lulu Direct integrates with Shopify and WooCommerce (and has an API).

Lulu Direct does standard sizes. For years they did not offer 5 x 8" but introduced this size in late

2022. Lulu Direct offers perfect binding (paperback), case-bound (hardcover), linen wrap (hardcover), and coil bound.

The quality of Lulu Direct books is excellent and their customer service is good.

You don't need your own ISBN to sell print with Lulu Direct.

Lulu Direct charges a $1.75 USD fulfilment fee per order.

Shipping.

Before i explain this, I must note that the 'Shopify Plan' referred to following is priced midway between the Shopify Basic Plan and the Shopify Advanced Plan.

For Lulu Direct on Shopify, you do not have to list manual shipping rates if you enable Third Party Carrier Calculated Shipping Rates. You do this either by 1) paying for any Shopify plan at the minimum level of the Shopify Plan 1 year in advance ($79 USD/month if paid annually) or by paying for that plan monthly ($105 USD/month when paid monthly) plus paying an extra monthly fee for Third Party Carrier Calculated Shipping

Rates. You then go on Shopify chat to request Third Party Shipping Rates. However, this is expensive, so it's much cheaper to offer manual rates. This means you have to set all the shipping rates.

With BookVault, you do not need to worry about entering shipping rates as they rates are downloaded to your store automatically when you download the app. Then you don't have to calculate shipping at all - it's all done automatically. Completely hands off for you!

HOW GETTING PAID WORKS.

If you sell print through a third party print provider (such as Lulu Direct or BookVault) app/plugin on Shopify or WooCommerce, this is how the payment works.

This assumes you are using the third party print provider's shipping rates, which means your store is set up to charge the customer exactly what the print provider charges to ship. The customer pays for shipping, and this goes directly to the third party print provider.

I will call the fictional customer Mary Smith. I've mentioned Mary before, but I'll mention her again for the sake of clarity. Who doesn't like clarity!

Mary Smith buys a $15 print book from your store and pays $5 for shipping.

$20 (the sale price of $15 plus the shipping cost of $5) goes into your account at once and is paid to you at whatever payment interval you have selected (daily, weekly, monthly—can be different for different countries—and also depends on your storefront). BookVault or Lulu Direct will take the money from your bank account for their costs (printing and shipping). If the printer app's costs are $10 ($5 for printing + $5 for shipping), you are $5 in profit.

Both Lulu Direct and BookVault have your payment method on file and debit it as needed.

TO SUM UP.

If you want books printed and shipped for you, use BookVault or Lulu Direct.

If you want to take orders personally from customers and then physically submit the order to a site instead of having it done automatically between the customer and the site, you could use BookVault, Amazon author copies, or IngramSpark.

However, if you are building a business, it is not a good idea to send a customer an Amazon author copy with Amazon branding all over it. Even books you buy from the Amazon retail store mention Amazon in the back.

RESOURCES

QUESTIONS

What is more important to you when selling print books: time or money?

Which method of selling print will you choose?

RESOURCES

Lulu Direct

Shopify apps.shopify.com/lulu-direct

WooCommerce help.luludirect.lulu.com/en/support/solutions/64000160418

API assets.lulu.com/media/guides/en/lulu-api-getting-started-guide.pdf

BookVault

Shopify bookvault.app/shopify/

WooCommerce bookvault.app/woocommerce/

API api.bookvault.app/v2/docs

Acutrack

Shopify apps.shopify.com/acutrack

WooCommerce
woocommerce.com/vendor/acutrack/

Other ecommerce integrations acutrack.com/test-integration/

Aerio

Website: aer.io

25. ACCEPTING PAYMENTS

66 Ecommerce isn't the cherry on the
cake, it's the new cake.

— JEAN PAUL AGON, FORMER CEO
L'OREAL

FRAUD PROTECTION.

When you accept payments, check first to see what
fraud prevention your storefront offers or you
might find yourself in a real pickle.

If your storefront or payment option does not
offer fraud protection as standard, consider paying
for it. Stripe Chargeback Protection, for example,
costs 0.4% per transaction. In the case of a fraudulent dispute, Stripe will cover the disputed

amount and waive any dispute fees without requiring any evidence to be submitted. Payhip, for example, offers Stripe as a payment option, so it's a good idea to look into this if you use Payhip.

PAYPAL

Most storefronts offer PayPal as a payment option. When you sign up for PayPal for Digital Goods with micropayments (for items under the price of around $10, depending on y0ur country) you're charged either standard fees or micropayments fees, whichever is the lower rate for each digital goods transaction, IF your country has PayPal Dynamic Pricing. if it doesn't, all your sales will attract the micropayment fee.

The PayPal micropayment rate is 5% + $0.05 AUD per transaction for domestic payments and 5.5% + $0.05 AUD for cross-border payments.

Unless you are in Austria or Belgium, if you have both Shopify Payments and PayPal enabled, Shopify will not take a cent from you when a customer pays with PayPal (or any additional payment method such as one of their approved cryptocurrency payment gateways).

If you don't have Shopify Payments enabled, Shopify will charge you extra fees. (2% on the

Shopify basic plan.) Shopify Payments are available to Australia, Austria, Belgium, Canada, Denmark, France, Germany, Hong Kong SAR, Ireland, Italy, Japan, Netherlands, New Zealand, Singapore, Spain, Sweden, United Kingdom, and the United States.

If somebody pays with Shop Pay (Shopify's default payment system) or other forms of payment under the Shopify Payments banner, Shopify charges credit card transaction fees. On the basic plan, this ranges from 1.75 to 2.9%, plus 30c, depending on your country.

Therefore, PayPal works out much cheaper for digital sales under the cut-off amount - IF your country has PayPal Dynamic Pricing. (Micropayment upper level cut off rate depends on your country/currency, usually $10-$12.)

If you look at the below graphic of the two examples, you can see the difference between a PayPal charge and a Shopify charge on a 99c item.

I ran an experiment to show the difference and set the price to 99c. I asked 2 relatives in the US to buy the book, 1 via PayPal and 1 via ShopPay.

PayPal charged me 12c AUD (with micropayments enabled).

This left me with $1.22 AUD.

$1.34 AUD	-$0.12	**$1.22**

This is what Shopify's ShopPay charged me. Not only was their currency conversion worse than PayPal's, ShopPay also charged me 35c, leaving me with $0.95 AUD.

I was 27c AUD per sale worse off with Shopify's payment method.

That would be fine with a few sales, but not with hundreds of sales. However, you do not want to sell books so cheaply in your store. It's best to sell bundles.

Gross total	$0.99 USD
Converted total (conversion rate: 1.31)	A$1.30 AUD
Shopify Payments fee (2.9% + A$0.30)	-A$0.32 AUD
Shopify Payments fee GST	-A$0.02 AUD
Currency conversion fee (2%)	-A$0.01 AUD
Currency conversion fee GST	A$0.00 AUD
Net total	A$0.95 AUD

CRYPTO.

It used to be good to offer this as an additional payment option if your storefront allowed it, but at the current time it doesn't really matter. Shopify and WooCommerce will accept certain crypto payment providers. You will just have to jump through some hoops to provide your ID to a cryptocurrency payment provider and set up a wallet to receive payments.

Shopify.

Shopify accepts the following crypto payment providers, plus others:

Crypto.com. Accepts more than 250 currencies including Bitcoin, Ethereum, Dogecoin, Cardano, Polkadot.

Coinbase Commerce. Accepts several cryptocurrencies including Bitcoin, Bitcoin Cash, Ethereum, Dogecoin, Litecoin, DAI.

BitPay. Accepts 14 cryptocurrencies including Bitcoin, Bitcoin Cash, Bitcoin Lightning, Ethereum, and Dogecoin.

WooCommerce.

If you are with WooCommerce, you can accept payments in more cryptocurrencies. You will need one of the following plugins.

NowPayments Plugin.

WooCommerce BTCPay for WooCommerce V2 Plugin.

Blockonomics Plugin.

Commerce Coinbase For WooCommerce.

CoinPayments.

CoinGate.

TripleA for WooCommerce.

RESOURCES

QUESTIONS

Which payment methods will you accept?

RESOURCES

Stripe Chargeback Protection stripe.-
com/radar/chargeback-protection

26. PEN NAMES

> 66 Opportunity is missed by most people because it is dressed in overalls and looks like work.
>
> — THOMAS EDISON

If you have a pen name and you want to keep it <u>secret/private</u> (such as if you write children's books and your pen name writes erotica, or in my case, namely, I write paranormal and my pen name's audience isn't fond of paranormal), you will need 2 stores.

<u>Please read this chapter carefully</u>. I am <u>not</u> saying everybody with a pen name needs more than 1 store, only those with a pen name which is

secret/private. So then, unless you are happy to broadcast your pen name/s to the world and wish to have a single store for your multiple selves, you will need two stores—if more than two author names, one store for each pen name.

That means double (at least) the expense: the plan, the apps/plugins, and so on. There isn't a way around this. Still, each pen name's store should be income-producing. Shopify millionaires and billionaires have multiple stores, one for each product.

You can have as many stores as you like on Shopify, but they have to be under separate accounts. You can use the same email address to log in, if you wish. If you do sign up for a subsequent Shopify store with the same email and log-in as your first store, you can hop from store to store under a convenient dropdown box.

In good news, it's super easy to have the one Book-Vault or Lulu Direct account for all your stores, whatever your ecommerce platform. In not-so-good news, if you are on Shopify, you will still need to enable Third Party Carrier Shipping for your pen name's store, and this means either paying for your pen name's store a year in advance (it's considerably cheaper, at any rate!) or paying a monthly fee.

If you have a separate store for your pen name, you will also need a separate BookFunnel account to deliver files (and for support) as you will need a separate webhook for each store.

RESOURCES

QUESTIONS

Will you have one store for all your pen names, or will you have separate store for your pen name/s? If so, will you do this immediately or wait until your main store is in profit?

RESOURCES

Book

Moonshots : Creating a World of Abundance, Naveen Jain, John Schroeter, Sir Richard Branson.

27. TRANSLATIONS

66 You can make a million excuses for why
something didn't go well, but ultimately,
just fix it and get on with it. Be a solu-
tions person.

— EMILY WEISS

You can sell your book translations in your main
store. You can set up different email flows based
on product purchase triggers. With Klaviyo, you
can set up the one email template to show French
content for customers located in France, for example, and then have English content for customers
elsewhere.

You can have a required language preference question on your newsletter signup forms and popups.

In Klaviyo, you can also change the language of the default, uneditable text. You will have to have the rest of the wording on the form translated into the target language, but if you have translations, you already have access to translators.

Klaviyo automatically segments subscribers based on location.

Shopify will translate the notification email into the buyer's own language automatically, that is, if you haven't changed the HTML of their thank you autoresponder. (I show how to do this in my course.)

In late 2022, Shopify introduced Shopify Translate. Now, when you add a new language to your store, Shopify will automatically install the Translate & Adapt app. This will automatically translate 2 languages for free. That is, when the customer from a chosen country lands on your store, they see the store in their own language. Any more than 2 added languages, there is a charge, but it remains free if you provide the translations.

I have my German translations on my main site. I link to them from the Header menu. Right now, I have the buyers of German books segmented in Klaviyo.

It's against the law in Germany to price lower somewhere else unless the book has been published for longer than 18 months.

BookFunnel does provide support to readers in all languages. Some of the language on the landing pages is customisable, but some can't be edited. I've had the bits I can edit translated into German, and I have also had wording translated to explain the non-customisable segments. Of course, this applies to all languages.

There is a workaround for everything!

RESOURCES

QUESTIONS

Will you offer translations on your store?

If so, have you ordered the translations for your store's wording and the wording of support emails?

RESOURCES

Book

The Art of Impossible: A Peak Performance Primer, Steven Kotler.

28. SELLING ON SOCIAL

> What do you need to start a business?
> Three simple things: know your
> product better than anyone, know your
> customer, and have a burning desire to
> succeed.
>
> — DAVE THOMAS, FOUNDER OF
> WENDY'S

With Shopify, you can sell direct from Google, Facebook, Instagram, Pinterest, TikTok, and YouTube.

To access the Marketing section of your Shopify dashboard, click Marketing in the left navigation. The Marketing section shows the amount of traffic and sales generated by each of your marketing sources, whether paid or free. It shows you the number of sessions, the number of orders from marketing, the dollar amount of sales from marketing, and the cost of sales from marketing. (The cost of sales from marketing will be zero if you have not run paid ads.) It will also give you the online store conversion rate.

Facebook.

You can create a free store on Facebook, simply by linking Shopify with Facebook. Facebook does not like to include digital products in the store (strange but true—they changed their name to Meta but won't accept digital? Go figure!) but Facebook generally accepts bundles containing a physical product plus digital products.

Shopify Analytics tells you which products were sold from the free store and gives you the dollar value. It might be a nice surprise for you, as it all happens seamlessly without your involvement.

You can run Facebook ads from the Shopify dashboard, and when somebody buys a book through Facebook, the order tells you the sale was via Facebook.

Facebook ads run from your store are Sales ads (used to be called Conversion ads), not the Traffic ads with which most authors are familiar.

Facebook and Shopify make it easy to retarget people who have already visited your store or taken action, such as making a purchase.

Dynamic Product Ads (DPAs) on Facebook work with Shopify, WooCommerce, Magento, and BigCommerce.

DPAs automatically show the right products to your hot and cold audiences. DPAs automatically differentiate between customers who have already taken specific actions such as purchasing, and customers who have visited your store and not purchased.

Dynamic Product Ads are highly effective at converting people who have already interacted with your store into paying customers. For example, if someone has already visited your product page and has not bought, DPAs will show this customer ads for those products.

If someone has added a product to their cart but didn't buy, DPAs will show them ads for those products. If somebody has already bought, DPAs will show them ads for similar products.

This happens automatically (yay!) so you don't have to do anything to set it up.

You can also, thanks to the Facebook pixel which you activate in your store, exclude customers who have already bought certain products.

When selling on the retailers, I'm sure you mostly (or exclusively) use Facebook Traffic ads. Now you are selling direct, you will use Sales ads (used to be called Conversion ads). However, there is still a place for Traffic ads. If you are starting out with a store, you can use Traffic ads to drive customers to your store in order to collect their data. Then you can use that collected data to create effective Conversion Facebook ads that send people to your website to buy.

Sales ads do not rely on targeting in the same way that Traffic ads do.

I should mention that sales ads work for your own store not for a retailer you do not own or control. The reason people recommend traffic ads to authors is solely for selling on the retailers. Sales ads are a different kettle of fish, and you cannot bring your traffic ads knowledge to the table.

I'm sure you can see by now that all this is quite different and nothing like the Facebook ad methods for selling on the retailers.

Instagram.

After you integrate Instagram with your store, Instagram Shopping creates a shop on your Instagram profile. You can then tag your products in posts and stories. Customers can click on posts to view a tagged product and select View on Website to buy from your store.

Customers can also select View Shop on your Instagram profile to view all of your products on Instagram.

This is free.

You can also run Instagram ads through your Shopify dashboard.

Google app.

The Google Sales Channel automatically syncs your Shopify store products with the Google Merchant Centre. You can also create paid Google Smart Shopping campaigns which appear on Google-owned platforms.

Smart Shopping campaigns are designed to reach shoppers when they're searching for products like yours on Google.

To get started, sign in to your Google account and open the Google Merchant Centre. Click the + button and select Add a product feed.

Next, select Shopify as your source and enter your Shopify store URL. Click Connect to Shopify and Authorise access.

The Google Sales Channel will now sync your Shopify products with the Google Merchant Centre.

Once a product has been synced to the Google Merchant Centre, you can create a Google Smart Shopping campaign. In the Google Merchant Centre, click +Campaign and select Google Shopping Campaign.

Next, enter your campaign name, select the Google Shopping campaign type, set the Max CPC bid, choose the Targeting and Negative keywords, and select your Product Grouping.

You can also use the Product Grouping to create a new product group. Click Save.

Google will now ask you to enter your Merchant ID for your Google Merchant Centre. You can find this in the Google app on your Shopify dashboard.

Next, you can add a product to your Google Shopping campaign by clicking Add Product and selecting the product from your list of synced products. You can also upload a new image if you wish.

When you have finished adding products, click Save. The Google Sales Channel will now appear in your channel manager.

As you can see, the Google Sales Channel is nice and easy to use and is fully integrated with Shopify. It's a must-have for any ecommerce business looking to increase their sales using Google's powerful advertising platform.

Google does require that you have at least two contact methods (not including contact forms) such as an email address and mailing address.

Tip.

Google also requires that you have a Refund Policy and a Terms of Service (same as Terms and Conditions) in the Footer of your store. You should have these anyway - but, back to Google. Google does not recognise the Refund Policy and Terms of Service on many non-acquired-from Shopify themes and will prompt you to add these policies. If you do add them via their prompt, you will end up with 2 Refund Policies and 2 Terms and Conditions in your footer. Yes, I'm speaking from experience!

The solution is to click through to the apps' Support (as shown below on Shopify) and explain that you do have these policies. Send a screenshot of your footer.

Google Support can also be confused by the fact you have both your physical location and, for example, Lulu Direct's physical location listed in your store's back end. You might have to explain that too. Generally, their Support is excellent.

Another tip.

Remove your digital products from Google, or you will go in endless circles with not being approved.

TikTok.

It's hard to believe that just a few years ago, TikTok didn't exist. Now, it's one of the most popular social media platforms in the world, with over one billion monthly users. Unlike Facebook and Instagram, TikTok isn't yet pay-to-play to any significant degree, so if you want to market your business on TikTok, the most popular strategies include using popular hashtags, using influencers, and creating trend-driven organic content.

Authors starting stores are faced with a hard decision: should you market your store on TikTok? The answer is simple. It's a Yes! If you're a business owner and you're looking to garner new customers, then you have to be on TikTok. It's the best way to get your brand out to the world.

But there's more to TikTok marketing than simply making an account and posting a video or two. You need to have a strategy. Most business owners fail to understand that they need to create a strategy to attract new customers.

You will need to consider the most effective way to use hashtags when marketing on TikTok, how to use influencers to drive new customers to your store, and the best way to create organic TikTok content.

Don't use hashtags as an afterthought. Hashtags are an effective way of drawing in new clients and customers to your business. You can use hashtags to target specific demographics, or to find users who have interests related to your business.

When deciding on which hashtags to use, you have a couple of options:

You can use hashtags that are already used in your genre. For example, if you're a romance author, you might hashtag your posts with #romance #romancenovel #romancenovels #romancebooks #romancereads #romanceseries #romancenovelsarethebest.

You can also come up with more inventive hashtags. Just make sure you use a couple of those popular ones to help people find you!

TikTok syncs well with Instagram, despite the fact TikTok and Instagram work in different ways. There's a special Instagram link button on your TikTok profile page, and when you post a video on TikTok you can select to share it automatically to your Instagram feed or stories.

If you are on Shopify and have a TikTok For Business account, you can add a shopping tab to your TikTok profile. This allows you to sync your products, directly linking them to your online store for checkout.

Adding a shopping tab to your TikTok profile is a great way to drive traffic to your online store and to increase sales. By syncing your products with your TikTok account, you can make it easy for customers to buy your products without leaving the app.

Pinterest.

A word of warning—Pinterest can be quite funny about accepting stores. It can refuse your store based on the fact you have a popup, for example. If it does approve your store, it will automatically post all your products to your Pinterest, along with shoppable pins. This is all free.

In any case, if you're looking to grow your business on Pinterest, some businesses use a tool such as Tailwind which is also for Instagram.

Ruggable, a hugely successful Shopify store that sells washable rugs, reported around three and a half million hits each month over the last few months to their Pinterest. This was a direct result of using the Shopify integration.

You also have the option to advertise on Pinterest.

Pinterest states that 85% of people use Pinterest on mobile devices. Sound familiar? It's advisable to use photos with a portrait rather than a landscape aspect, which is fine as books are portrait aspect anyway.

YouTube.

In July 2022, YouTube announced a partnership with Shopify.

Now, a viewer can shop directly from YouTube. Sellers can connect their stores to YouTube and tag their own products in videos and live streams as well as pin products in live chat.

There is also a Store Tab which you can add to your YouTube channel to feature your products.

There are eligibility requirements for shopping, such as that the YouTube channel needs a minimum of 500 subscribers.

Bottom line: Creators with YouTube channels can sell products from their Shopify stores directly on YouTube.

Linkpop.

Shopify's Linkpop tool is a free link-in-bio tool that allows you to build a page of links for social media. It connects with your Shopify products, so you are able to sell your products through your Linkpop page using shoppable links. This way, your followers can click through to your products and buy them directly from your store.

RESOURCES

QUESTIONS

Have you linked your store with your socials?

TO DO

Make a list of free stores on socials.

Add LinkPop to your socials.

RESOURCES

Books

When the Miracle Drops: How Instagram Helped Turn a Quick Fix Into a Million-Dollar Product, Jessica Dupart.

Influence, New and Expanded: The Psychology of Persuasion, Robert B. Cialdini.

YouTube

YouTube on Shopify integration

blog.youtube/news-and-events/youtube-shopify-integration-merch-shopping/

29. SALES TAX

> A fine is a tax for doing something wrong. A tax is a fine for doing something right.

— ANONYMOUS

Disclaimer: This is for informational purposes only. It is not intended to replace professional advice. I am not a certified tax advisor. I am not a financial adviser. For further help, or if you are ever in doubt, please consult a professional tax advisor or accountant or tax authorities.

Sales tax!

Nobody likes it, but every single ecommerce business deals with it.

<u>Don't confuse sales tax with income tax</u>. The tax forms we have to file with retailers for receiving royalties are for income tax, not sales tax. Tax treaties between countries are for income tax, not sales tax.

Let's cut straight to the chase. Do you have to pay sales tax?

It depends where you live and where your customer lives, where your third party printer is located, and/or whether the goods you sell are digital (and whether they are ebooks or audio-books) or physical or subscriptions, and/or how many transactions you make in a certain time. I didn't say it was fun!

The good news is that it's not as bad as you think. Read to the end of the chapter for an easy solution. But don't skip ahead! You won't understand it if you do.

Unless you are in the USA and have physical nexus, the places you will likely have to register for sales tax at once are the EU and the UK. (Don't worry - there's a great app that will do it all for you.)

By the way, the third party book printer, Lulu Direct, collects and remits sales tax for you on books you print with them. And if you don't use Lulu Direct, please note that if you are a non-EU resident selling only print books into the EU, you don't have to do anything if you don't want to - the customer pays it.

Payhip collects and remits digital UK and EU VAT for you. (Note that sales of print books and ebooks to the UK are zero-rated for VAT.)

Shopify's dashboard tells you if, where, and when you have a tax obligation. Shopify Tax tells you if you have a tax obligation in the US. It tells you how much it is.

I strongly advise asking your accountant about sales tax in your own location. Note that most accountants are not au fait with international sales tax, that is, sales tax outside your own country, as this is highly specialist field.

Basically, you have three choices:

1. You figure it all out for yourself, register, and pay sales tax.

2. You get a tax app/plugin that remits tax for you.

3. You get a tax app/plugin that does everything apart from remitting tax for you but does tell you

how, when, and where to remit that tax and hand-holds you through the process.

Where might you need to pay sales tax once you make a bucketload of money?

Australia.

Let's get Australia out of the way first as it's straightforward. Unless you make $75,000 AUD in a 12 month period (in any or all states) from sales solely to Australia, you don't have to register for or pay sales tax (GST) in Australia.

Sales tax in Australia is 10%.

New Zealand.

The sales tax threshold for a 12 month period is $60,000 NZD.

Sales tax in New Zealand is 15%.

Canada.

The Canadian sales tax threshold for non-Canadians in a 12 month period is $30,000 CAD.

Canada has a federal consumption tax, GST/HST. In addition to that, some Canadian provinces have their own sales tax system (5%, 13%, or 15%). Five provinces have both federal and provincial sales taxes. This is known as the Harmonized Sales Tax (HST).

Note. Canada has certain provinces with a zero threshold for digital.

UK and EU VAT.

VAT is different for each EU country.

If you sell certain digital content to a customer (B2C) (that is, not to another business, B2B) in the EU, then you have to collect and pay VAT on every sale.

Books and ebooks in the UK are zero rated for VAT. (Audiobooks are a different matter.) If you sell audiobooks and/or non-ebook digital content to a customer (B2C) (that is, not to another business, B2B) in the UK, then you have to collect and pay VAT on every sale.

If your business is in the EU and you need to register, then you register for VAT in your own country. If you make less than €10,000 in cross-border EU sales of audiobooks and/or non-ebook digital content per year, then you charge your local tax rate to all customers and you file returns with your own country.

If you run a business outside of the EU, you can choose any EU country to host your tax registration. You must sign up with that country's One-Stop Shop (OSS). Many English speakers choose Ireland. You file returns quarterly online with the OSS where you're registered, and it passes the VAT along to the relevant locations.

Or, if your store is Shopify, WooCommerce, Magento, Wix, or Squarespace, you could simply get the EAS EU & UK Compliance app to do it all for you.

Is your head spinning already? The one main thing that prevents authors from selling direct is sales tax. Keep reading in order to feel better about it.

All ecommerce businesses have to deal with sales tax, but as authors with our low price, high volume books, some tax apps strike us a heavy blow. I've mentioned that some apps charge per 200 transactions. For example, Quaderno charges $49 USD a month for up to 250 transactions, then it's $99 USD a month. It doesn't take an author long to have more than 250 monthly transactions in their store.

However, you can exclude countries from your Quaderno plan, so if you're sure you're not close to economic nexus in the US and you don't have physical nexus in the US, you could simply exclude the US from the Quaderno plan. Check with Quaderno first.

TaxJar charges $19 USD a month for up to 200 orders with 4 free autofiles a year. TaxJar also charges $99 a month for up to 200 orders with 12 free autofiles a year.

Here's the thing: an author with 200 transactions might be making $1,000 from 200 transactions whereas a seller of other products might be making $20,000 from 200 transactions. That's quite a difference. It's hardly equitable, but that's the way the cookie crumbles.

When you're paying a lot for a tax app, you want to get one with good support. Check the negative reviews on all tax apps and see if there is a consensus of opinion.

Another sales tax app (the one I use) is EAS EU & UK Compliance which is for UK and EU VAT. It automates the EU VAT reports, and you can choose whether to do the filing or let EAS EU do the filing. The prices range from 0,32€ per transaction (you file) to 1,25€ per transaction (they file). Clearly then, it's not a good idea to put an audio-book on sale for 99c (or 0,99€) if using this app.

The EAS EU & UK Compliance app is ideal if you are selling print books to the EU and you prefer to pay VAT rather than leaving it to the customer to pay. You do not need to register with the IOSS for VAT for print books to the EU, but it's a good idea to do so to avoid hassles for your EU customers.

I myself use the EAS EU & UK Compliance app. The app people will install it on your site for free and set up everything on your site for you - all for free. They will also register you with the IOSS for free - and this is something that normally requires an agent and is expensive, so big savings there!

You can also have EAS EU & UK Compliance register you with the OSS for EU digital VAT and remit your sales tax for you. I registered with the HMRC for UK VAT (it takes around 20 minutes and was the easiest tax form I'd ever had to fill out, although their follow-up questions can be highly tedious to wade though), and I have EAS EU & UK Compliance file the UK VAT for me. (Remember, time is money!)

I use the third party printer BookVault in the UK to print and ship my books, and I provide Book-Vault with my VAT numbers.

I know it's a lot to take in, but it really is straight-forward. You just have to know where your obligations are.

The bottom line is this.

There are 3 main places you might be liable to register for sales tax soon after you start your store: 1. US (**if** you have physical nexus in the US) 2. UK 3. EU if you sell digital content. Still, be sure to check the list of countries below because if you sell even one ebook to certain countries, you have to register for VAT in that country. You can exclude those (or any) countries from most sales platforms, so there's no need to worry.

USA.

If you have **physical nexus** in the US, you have to pay sales tax. That means you live, have a ware-house, an office, use a fulfilment centre, or have another qualifying presence in a US state that has sales tax. "Shopify Tax" can help tell you where your physical nexus obligations are.

If you live anywhere in the world, inside or outside the US (and don't have a qualifying presence in a US state that has sales tax), you only have to pay sales tax **when (if)** you reach **economic nexus**.

There are 23 US states that do not tax digital products. Those that do, charge between 1% and 7%.

US States with Economic Nexus for Digital Products, Thresholds (in a 12 month period).

Alabama $250,000

Arizona $100,000

Arkansas $100,000 or 200 transactions

Colorado $100,000

Connecticut $2000,000 and 200 transactions

Hawaii $200,000 or 200 transactions

Idaho $100,000

Indiana $100,000 or 200 transactions

Iowa $100,000

Kentucky $100,000 or 200 transactions

Louisiana $100,000 or 200 transactions

Maine $100,000

Maryland $100,000 or 200 transactions

Minnesota $100,000 or 200 transactions

Mississippi $250,000

Nebraska $100,000 or 200 transactions

New Jersey $100,000 or 200 transactions

New Mexico $100,000

North Carolina $100,000 or 200 transactions

Ohio $100,000 or 200 transactions

Pennsylvania $100,000

Puerto Rico $100,000 or 200 transactions

South Carolina $100,000

South Dakota $100,000 or 200 transactions

Tennessee $100,000

Texas $500,000

Utah $100,000 or 200 transactions

Vermont $100,000 or 200 transactions

Washington $100,000

Washington DC $100,000 or 200 transactions

Wisconsin $100,000

Wyoming $100,000 or 200 transactions

So you can see that the dollar value thresholds won't be achieved overnight, although 200 transactions could be achieved far more readily. Keep an eye on your transaction numbers to these states: Arkansas, Hawaii, Indiana, Kentucky, Louisiana, Maryland, Minnesota, Nebraska, New Jersey, North Carolina, Ohio, Puerto Rico, South Dakota, Utah, Vermont, Washington, and Wyoming. If you have Shopify, it will let you know.

Some other countries' VAT for NON residents of that country.

Albania.

Their threshold is 0. That's right, zero. Sellers must register as soon as they sell anything to Albania. VAT is 20%.

Algeria.

Yes, another zero threshold. Sellers must register as soon as they sell anything to Algeria. Their VAT is 10%.

Armenia.

Armenia's sales tax threshold is 115 million AMD.

Angola.

No registration threshold and 14% VAT.

Bahamas.

Their registration threshold is BSD 100,000 and VAT is 12%.

Bahrain.

No registration threshold and 10% VAT.

Bangladesh.

Their registration threshold is BDT 30M and VAT is 15%.

Belarus.

No registration threshold and 20% VAT.

Cambodia.

Their registration threshold is KHR 250 million and VAT is 10%.

Cameroon.

Their registration threshold is XAF 50 million and VAT is 19.5%.

Chile.

No registration threshold and 19% VAT.

Colombia.

No registration threshold and 18% VAT.

Côte d'Ivoire.

No registration threshold and 18% VAT.

Egypt.

Egypt's registration threshold is EGP 500,000 and VAT is 14%.

Iceland.

Iceland's registration threshold is 2.000.000 ISK with a VAT of 22.5% apart from ebooks which are charged a VAT of 11%.

India.

No registration threshold and 18% VAT (5% for ebooks).

Indonesia.

Their registration threshold is IDR 600,000,000 and VAT is 11%.

Japan.

Japan's annual threshold for this tax is JPY 10 million and VAT is 10%.

Kazakhstan.

No registration threshold and 12% VAT.

Kenya.

No registration threshold and 16% VAT.

Kosovo.

No registration threshold and 18% VAT.

Kyrgyzstan.

No registration threshold and 12% VAT.

Laos.

Their registration threshold is LAK 400 million and their VAT is 10%.

Malaysia.

The registration threshold is RM 500,000 and VAT is 6%.

Mexico.

No registration threshold. VAT is 16% for all foreign sellers, and you must sign up for VAT through a local representative. Mexico requires you to file monthly.

Nigeria.

No registration threshold and 7.5% VAT.

Norway.

The registration threshold is NOK 50,000 and the VAT is 25%. No VAT for ebooks!

Russia.

No registration threshold and 20% VAT (10% for ebooks and audiobooks).

Saudi Arabia.

No registration threshold and 15% VAT.

Serbia.

No registration threshold and 20% VAT.

Singapore.

Singapore has 2 different thresholds: the seller's annual global turnover must exceed SGD $1,000,000 (around $760,000 USD) and the sale of digital services to Singapore consumers exceeds SGD $100,000.

South Africa.

The registration threshold is ZAR 1,000,000 (around $56,000 USD) and 14% VAT.

South Korea.

No registration threshold and 10% VAT.

Switzerland.

Their registration threshold is CHF 100,000 (around $108,000 USD) in global sales and VAT is 7.7% (2.5% for physical books and ebooks).

Taiwan.

Their registration threshold is NTD 480,000 and VAT is 5%.

Thailand.

The registration threshold is THB 1.8 million and VAT is 7%.

Tunisia.

No registration threshold and 19% VAT.

Turkey.

No registration threshold and 18% VAT.

Uganda.

No registration threshold and 18% VAT.

Ukraine.

Their registration threshold is UAH 1 million for the preceding calendar year. VAT is 20%.

United Arab Emirates.

No registration threshold and 5% VAT.

Uzbekistan.

No registration threshold and 10% VAT.

Vietnam.

No registration threshold and 10% VAT.

It depends where you live and where your customer lives. Location, location, location does not apply solely to real estate!

It is better to err on the side of caution. If in doubt, either exclude the country, or register for sales tax, or use an app. And take heart! When you sell direct, you are running a business, and every ecommerce business deals with sales tax.

Here is what to do.

Sales tax for your own country.

Your accountant will advise you.

Sales tax outside your own country.

The way to cope with UK and EU VAT (digital and physical goods) is the EAS EU & UK Compliance app. As I said, they will install it and set it up on your store for free. They will remit your sales tax for you.

Avoid selling to certain countries.

With some storefronts such as Shopify, you can choose not to sell to countries with zero VAT thresholds such as India.

Don't avoid all countries, though. With Australia, for example, you need to make over $70,000 AUD worth of sales to/in Australia in a single year before you have to register for sales tax.

There is also a good app (currently $3.99 a month) with which you can exclude countries, states, or provinces.

RESOURCES

QUESTIONS

Have you made a list of your main markets?

How will you handle sales tax? Will you do it yourself or use an app/plugin?

RESOURCES

Quaderno has a free sales tax calculator:

www.quaderno.io/vat-calculator

How to register and file taxes in the UK:

www.quaderno.io/tax-registration-filing-guides/uk

APPENDIX: POLICIES FOR THE FOOTER

> 66 This is not exciting reading, but it's necessary.
>
> — I SAID THIS!

Disclaimer: This information is not legal advice. Check with a lawyer. I am not a lawyer. Also, ascertain the laws specific to your country.

In your store's Footer, you do need the following policies:

Privacy Policy
Terms and Conditions
Refund Policy
Shipping Policy.

(Not a policy, but it's a good idea to have FAQs in your Footer as well.)

Your country will likely have companies that offer policy generators online. Most come with a free plan of around a week, so you can edit your policies while on the free plan. You can tweak the policies to suit your business.

There will be some overlap between the policies—it's fine to repeat information.

In my course, I also provide comprehensive policies you can copy and edit.

Privacy Policy.

If you collect information from customers (such as names, addresses, and credit card numbers), your Privacy Policy should disclose the ways in which you use that information. You should also explain why you need information and with whom you share it.

This should also include an easy-to-understand cookie policy.

You include all your email marketing and SMS marketing disclosure information here, especially in relation to GDPR requirements.

It doesn't matter if you don't live in the UK or in an EU country. If you collect the email or personal data of a single customer who lives in the UK or EU, you have to be GDPR-compliant. This is no surprise to authors. Make sure you stick all your GDPR-compliant here in your Privacy Policy.

Strict rules apply to SMS marketing, so make sure you cover them in your privacy policy. Express consent is required for SMS marketing, so explicitly state that you will not share the data with any third parties.

State what you do with the phone numbers you collect and how you use them.

If you have an SMS abandoned cart flow, you need to state how your website captures that information to determine when a customer's cart has been abandoned. Is it cookies or a plugin? Mention this in your policy.

If it is cookies, state that your site uses cookies to track items the customer has abandoned in their cart and to determine when to send cart reminder messages via SMS.

Terms and Conditions.

This policy should provide your contact information.

It's a good idea to start this policy with wording like: "By using this Site, you indicate that you have read and understood these Terms and Conditions and agree to abide by them at all times."

It should address the following:

Agreement to emails

Intellectual Property

Acceptable Use

(Do not Violate the intellectual property rights of the Site owners)

Accounts

(When you create an account on our Site, you agree to the following:…)

Sale of Goods

(Mention the goods available on your Site)

Payments

(Mention the payment methods you accept)

Shipping and Delivery

(When you purchase goods from our Site, the goods will be delivered through one of the following methods:…)

Refunds

(Refunds for Goods)

(Refunds for Digital items)

(Mention whether refunds apply to Digital goods.)

Limitation of Liability

Indemnity

Additional Terms

Changes

(Mention that the Terms and Conditions may be amended from time to time.)

Contact Details

Refund Policy.

Your Refund Policy should state your store's return policies and your refund policies.

Sure, you already mentioned them in Terms and Conditions, but mention them again here.

Do you offer a refund for digital goods? Explain your policy here.

Some people have said to me that they don't offer refunds so they don't have a refund policy. Still, you need a refund policy which states you don't accept refunds. This is business, and you have to act like business.

Shipping Policy.

Your Shipping Policy should include the following information:

What shipping options you offer

How long you take to ship an order

Any restrictions you might have on shipping

How you pack your products.

Also, mention digital delivery here - again!

MY COURSE FOR AUTHORS
SELLING DIRECT

Learn from somebody who has been doing it since 1993!

I teach sound ecommerce principles, not 'special schemes' or unusual methods–rather, tried and true ecommerce methods.

I offer a hugely comprehensive Teachable course, Authors Selling on Shopify. Find out more here by typing this in your browser: https://best-business-for-authors.teachable.com/p/authors-selling-on-shopify

There are numerous modules and over 100 lectures.

There's a private Facebook group solely for people who enrol in the course.

After enrolling, you have unlimited access to the course for as long as the course is available. You also have free access to all updates. The course is updated constantly to take account of changes with Shopify and the industry.

The course is self-paced and online. Learn in your own time. You are able to download all the course notes.

This bundle course has 3 courses. Save by doing the bundle!.

1. Simply Shopify Pro.

2. Klaviyo Ecommerce Email and SMS marketing. (This extensive module has step-by-step tutorials for all flows.)

3. Facebook Ads for Ecommerce. (This comprehensive module has step-by-step tutorials for Sales ads - nothing like Traffic ads for retailers! You will learn how to run ads which are specific to ecommerce.)

NOTES

5. WHAT YOU CAN DO WITH A STORE

1. https://www.cnbc.com/2022/02/02/facebook-says-apple-ios-privacy-change-will-cost-10-billion-this-year.html

8. WHY SELL DIRECT? THE BENEFITS!

1.

13. IMPROVING STORE SPEED

1. Google Data, Global, n=3,700 aggregated, anonymized Google Analytics data from a sample of mWeb sites opted into sharing benchmark data, March 2016.

15. TOKENGATING AND NFTS

1. https://twitter.com/Shopify/status/1503450544387633153

17. LET'S GET LEGAL!

1. https://sellercentral.amazon.com/gp/help/external/
   G201972160?language=en_US

ABOUT THE AUTHOR

 USA Today Bestselling author, Morgana Best, started selling print direct in 1993 and ebooks (as well as print) direct from her websites in 2003. In 2007, indie authors turned to the retailers, but now the tide is turning back to selling direct.

Morgana Best is the founder of Authors Selling Direct™

authorssellingdirect.com

https://best-business-for-authors.teachable.-com/p/authors-selling-on-shopify

WS - #0019 - 120424 - C1 - 203/127/19 - PB - 9781922595713 - Matt Lamination